Conscientious Objectors of the Second World War

Conscientious Objectors of the Second World War

Refusing to Fight

Ann Kramer

PEN & SWORD
SOCIAL HISTORY

First published in Great Britain in 2013 by
Pen & Sword Social History
an imprint of
Pen & Sword Books Ltd
47 Church Street
Barnsley
South Yorkshire
S70 2AS

Hardback 978-1-84468-118-1

Typeset in 11pt Ehrhardt by
Mac Style, Beverley, E. Yorkshire

Printed and bound in the UK by CPI Group (UK) Ltd, Croydon, CRO 4YY

Pen & Sword Books Ltd incorporates the Imprints of Pen & Sword
Aviation, Pen & Sword Family History, Pen & Sword Maritime, Pen &
Sword Military, Pen & Sword Discovery, Wharncliffe Local History,
Wharncliffe True Crime, Wharncliffe Transport, Pen & Sword Select, Pen
& Sword Military Classics, Leo Cooper, The Praetorian Press, Remember
When, Seaforth Publishing and Frontline Publishing.

For a complete list of Pen & Sword titles please contact
PEN & SWORD BOOKS LIMITED
47 Church Street, Barnsley, South Yorkshire, S70 2AS, England
E-mail: enquiries@pen-and-sword.co.uk
Website: www.pen-and-sword.co.uk

Contents

Acknowledgements

Thanks are due to the following:

Susannah Farley-Green for permission to quote from an interview with her about her father, Eric Farley, and from his unpublished memoir, *A Partial View*, also for permission to reproduce photographs and memorabilia belonging to the family.

Lorna Vahey for permission to quote from an interview with her about her father, Fred Vahey, to quote from his memoirs and for permission to reproduce photographs and memorabilia belonging to the family.

Jenny Foot & Gwylim Newnham for permission to quote from an interview with them about their father, Jack Newnham.

Martin Davies for permission to quote from his account of service with the FAU (BBC People's War).

Ifanwy Williams, for permission to quote from an interview with her about her experience of registering as a CO.

Sally Phillips for permission to quote from an interview with her father Brian Phillips, who sadly died before this book was finished.

Isle of Man Newspapers Ltd for permission to quote from *The Objectors: personal stories of five conscientious objectors* (Times Press and Anthony Gibbs & Phillips, 1965). Specifically extracts from personal accounts by Clifford Simmons, Sydney Carter and Stuart Smith.

Merlin Press Ltd for permission to quote from *Human Guinea-Pigs*, by Kenneth Mellanby (Merlin Press, 1973).

The Peace Pledge Union for permission to quote from *Challenge of Conscience* by Denis Hayes (Allen & Unwin, 1949); *Peace News*, the PPU website, and *Peace News* and for permission to reproduce photographs.

The Board of Trustees of the Fellowship of Reconciliation for kind permission to reproduce photographs of COs working on the land with the Christian Pacifist Forestry and Land Units (CPFLU).

The Co-operative Women's Guild for permission to quote from *The Guildswoman*, May 1939.

Mrs Marjatta Bryan for permission to quote extracts from Alex Bryan's book: *"Bloody conchie!": a conscientious objector looks back to World War Two* (Quaker Books, 1986).

Mrs Rosalie Huzzard for permission to quote extracts from R. Huzzard's private papers held in the Imperial War Museum Documents Department.

Mrs Winifred Porcas for permission to quote extracts from R.J. Porcas's private papers held in the Imperial War Museum Documents Department.

The Imperial War Museum Documents Department for assistance in tracing copyright holders of documents used. Every effort has been made to trace copyright holders and the author and the Imperial War Museum would be grateful for any information which might help to trace those whose identities or addresses are not currently known.

Reproduced with permission of Curtis Brown Group Ltd, London on behalf of The Trustees of the Mass Observation Archive. Copyright © The Trustees of the Mass Observation Archive.

Every attempt has been made to contact the copyright holders of quoted materials. Should any references have been omitted, please supply details to the publisher, who will endeavour to correct the information in subsequent editions.

Introduction

People of Conscience

It is hard to believe today just how much the Second World War permeated the early lives of those who were born immediately after it, as I was. Rationing, austerity, bombsites and prefabs were part of the landscape when I was a child in North London. So was the awareness, if not the understanding, that the previous generation had just gone through six years of war. My family did not promote force or fighting but both my parents had served in the war – my father as a doctor, in the Royal Army Medical Corps and my mother as a nurse with the Voluntary Aid Detachment (VAD). Separately they were posted to India, where they met and married. Their wartime roles were to mend bodies not destroy them and they did not glorify war. Yet, from what I gathered, they clearly believed that the war was one that had to be fought, that it was as many believed a 'just' war, and for the first few years of my life it never occurred to me to question this. I accepted it. I had no idea that there was an alternative view, nor did I know that a huge number of people during the Second World War had, for very principled reasons, refused to fight.

I don't know when I first began to question the need for war, perhaps once I knew about the horrors of Hiroshima and Nagasaki, but at some point I realised that for me war was an unacceptable and futile way of trying to solve problems. By the time I was 14 or 15, I had joined the Campaign for Nuclear Disarmament (CND). I went on Aldermaston marches; demonstrated against the Vietnam War; and protested at Greenham Common. I carried on demonstrating – against the bombing of Libya in 1987; against the first Iraq conflict; and again in 2003 with the two million or more who marched against the government's decision to invade Iraq. It was what I did and it was what my friends were doing. So, while I grew up in a home where my parents had taken part in a war, my daughter grew up in a home where people were constantly making placards or arranging to go on yet another anti-war demonstration.

Ironically for someone who has been involved in anti-war activities, I have written a great deal about the two world wars in the last few years, both for children and adults. One of the things I've noticed is just how little has been written about people who have taken a principled stand against war to the extent of refusing to take up arms, compared with those involved in war, both on the home front or on the battlefield. It is fascinating stuff and very valid, although conventionally it is those who participate in war who are highlighted, while those who take the immensely courageous step of resisting the call to war receive very little coverage.

War memorials alone make this point: just about every town and village has a memorial honouring the dead of both wars. Yet pacifists and conscientious objectors have very few and their memorials have only been created fairly recently. In 1994 Michael Tippett, then president of the Peace Pledge Union, unveiled a huge slate memorial to conscientious objectors past and present in London's Tavistock Square. The Peace Pledge Union co-ordinated its creation and today it is a focus for events on and around International Conscientious Objectors' Day, 15 May, when COs are remembered, not just in London, but all around the world. International Conscientious Objectors' Day was not observed until 1982. In Wales, where there is a long tradition of pacifism, the first memorial to conscientious objectors was unveiled as recently as 2005. It stands in Cardiff, in the National Garden of Peace.

Not only do pacifists and conscientious objectors get relatively little attention, but also the conscientious objectors of the Second World War have until recently remained in the shadow of those of the First World War. This is not really surprising, as the story of the First World War conscientious objectors, who numbered about 16,000, is a very dramatic one. These were the first conscientious objectors in Britain. Their trailblazing stand against conscription and war came at a time when jingoism was at its height and thousands of young men were being slaughtered in the trenches. It meant that they were vilified to an appalling extent.

Twenty years later, during the Second World War, well over 60,000 men and around 1,000 women in Britain took the decision to register as conscientious objectors and claim exemption from military service. They refused to fight or to undertake war-related work as a matter of conscience. They came from different backgrounds and social classes and their reasons for swimming against the national tide of war and militarism also varied. But however different they were as people, they all shared one basic belief, that it was wrong, whether for religious, moral, political or humanitarian reasons, to be conscripted for war and to take up arms and fight, no matter how great the danger facing Britain, no matter how much pressure was put on them to change their minds.

Largely because of the courage and determination of First World War COs, attitudes towards and treatment of conscientious objectors during the Second World War were more humane and tolerant than they had been 20 years previously. Even so, it was not easy to be a conscientious objector during the Second World War. The personal costs were very high: conscientious objectors lost their jobs; many were abused; some were ostracised; others were brutalised and many went to prison. There was also a social stigma attached to being a conscientious objector that in some cases lasted until well after the war – hence so few memorials and the lack of recognition outside the peace movement.

It has also been said that, given the awfulness of Nazism and Fascism, it was harder to be a conscientious objector between 1939–45 than it had been in 1916–18. Many of the accounts I have read during my research bear this out, providing evidence of considerable soul-searching and anxiety. Deciding to refuse conscription taxed the consciences of some to the very limit; proof of which perhaps is the fact that some long-term pacifists renounced their principles and joined up when war began. Interestingly, one of the things I had not quite realised before I began this book is that 'pacifism' and 'conscientious objection' are not necessarily one and the same thing. Strictly, conscientious objection is a legal status conferred on someone who refuses conscription on grounds of conscience, pacifism is a doctrine or belief system. Many, though not all, conscientious objectors were pacifists, while not all pacifists became conscientious objectors.

Either way it took immense courage to be a conscientious objector during the Second World War and to maintain that stand throughout six long years of war. Many COs had worked hard to prevent war before it happened, and, as thoughtful people with social consciences, they knew the horrors of Nazism but they believed profoundly that war and taking up arms was not the right way. Therefore, when the time came, they took another very principled stand. In the words of Gwylim Newnham, whose father was a Second World War conscientious objector, 'their stories deserve to be better known'.

I need to thank many people who have helped me in writing this book. First and foremost Bill Hetherington and the Peace Pledge Union, who have allowed me to haunt their offices and to spend time going through their archives. Bill is the PPU's archivist and has been for many years compiling a database of conscientious objectors from both world wars. He probably knows more about conscientious objectors than just about anybody else. When I started, everyone told me he was the man to contact and he has never failed to answer my numerous questions and to put me on the right track. I am immensely grateful to him. If I've introduced any errors, they are entirely my fault, not his.

I also want to thank Susannah Farley-Green and Lorna Vahey, both of whose fathers were conscientious objectors during the Second World War. They have generously shared information about their fathers and have given me permission to use extracts from their memoirs as well as photographs. I was fortunate enough to know Fred and Zoe Vahey; they were the first conscientious objectors I had met and were remarkable people. I did not know Eric Farley but his memoirs are a joy to read. Thanks also to Sally Phillips, who arranged an interview for me with her father, Brian Phillips. Sadly Brian died before this book was finished but he was a most impressive man, who gave me an insight into the peace and pacifism of Quakerism. My thanks as well to Jenny Foot and Gwylim Newnham who allowed me to interview them about their father Jack Newnham. I am very grateful to friends and colleagues in the peace movement, such as Phil Steele, Emily Johns, Milan Rai and John Lynes, who provided suggestions, leads and general support. Thanks to Phil, I was able to interview Ifanwy Williams in Wales, which was a bonus. As always staff at the Imperial War Museum have been enormously helpful and their resources are invaluable. I have only been able to interview a few conscientious objectors, but the sound archives at the Imperial War Museum contain a fascinating collection of interviews. These have been of great help and enabled me at least to hear the voices of conscientious objectors.

I am grateful to Martin Davies, who allowed me to use extracts from his account of life in the Friends Ambulance Unit and thanks, but also apologies, to Angela Sinclair Loutit. We made three attempts to conduct an interview and, although in her nineties, she is still so politically active that somehow the interview never quite happened. I would like to thank the Authors' Foundation who kindly provided me with a grant to complete this book. It has been enormously useful. I am also grateful to Pen and Sword Books, my publishers, who accepted the idea for this book and have waited patiently for me to finish it. Finally I want to thank friends and family, but particularly my partner Marcus Weeks, for their support and encouragement.

Chapter 1

A Flourishing Peace Movement

'I renounce war, and never again, directly or indirectly, will I sanction or support another'

Peace Pledge Union

When Fred Vahey was a young boy of about five or six, he was puzzled by the sight of what he later described as 'a lot of ill people all over the town in pale blue soft clothes – many on crutches or with bandages, or missing limbs. There seemed to be a strange air about it all ... these sick wrecks had survived ... from some outrageous thing that I did not understand.'

Later Fred came to understand that the 'outrageous thing' was the First World War, and the 'sick wrecks' were casualties. He never forgot the sight. Born in Ireland in 1910 the experience caused him to question the whole purpose and value of war – not just the First World War but of all wars. In 1940, arguing that war 'is a crime against humanity' and conscription 'a denial of human liberty', Fred registered as a conscientious objector and refused to take any part in the war effort. He spent the war years working on his smallholding and until his death in 1996 remained steadfastly opposed to war, never doubting his decision to take a conscientious stand against it.

Fred Vahey was not the only person to renounce war during what Robert Graves called 'The Long Weekend' – the brief space between 1919–1939 that separated the two world wars. Thousands of others also did so. The First World War had caused unprecedented devastation and loss of life. Some ten million young men had died in the trenches, more than twice that number had been wounded and about six million civilians had been killed. Families in all the warring countries mourned the loss of husbands, fiancés, brothers, uncles, friends and lovers. In Britain, France and Germany virtually an entire generation of young men had been wiped out. Announcing the end of fighting to the House of Commons on 11 November 1918, the then British Prime Minister David Lloyd George described the First World War as 'the cruellest and most terrible war that has ever scourged mankind'; years later in 1934 the Hastings Peace Group estimated that it would have taken three months for 'the vast army who died as a direct or indirect result of the war ... marching day and night at the rate of four per second' to have passed the doors of the White Rock Pavilion on Hastings seafront.

Widespread revulsion

Exhaustion, relief and victory parades marked the arrival of peace, and memorials to the 'glorious dead' were erected in towns and villages throughout Britain. In 1921 the first Armistice Day Remembrance Ceremony was held at the Cenotaph in London's Whitehall. According to *The Times*, a 'countless multitude' attended the ceremony, which was intended not just to commemorate 'the sacrifice and suffering of war' but also the 'winning of victory and the dawn of peace'. Interestingly, that same day some 200 delegates from Britain's leading women's organisations met at 8.30pm in Central Hall, Westminster, to demonstrate their support for a reduction in armaments. Key speakers included Lady Astor MP, trade unionist Margaret Bondfield and suffragist Maude Royden.

Given the scale of death and destruction it was hardly surprising that when the post-war dust finally settled, there was a widespread revulsion against war and militarism. This manifested in various ways, not least in a large and unprecedented peace movement that flourished during the inter-war period. It is difficult to estimate the numbers actively involved, but while most people in Britain just hoped that war would not happen again, tens of thousands, many of whom described themselves as pacifists, joined anti-war or pacifist organisations and campaigned in one way or another for peace. Then as now, pacifists, or those who thought they were pacifists, were a minority of the population, but they were certainly a sizeable minority. Their numbers were sufficiently significant by the mid to late 1930s for some people to accuse pacifists of helping Hitler's war aims.

The inter-war peace movement attracted a whole range of people. They included scientists, artists, musicians, politicians, clerks, students, activists and thinkers. There were high-profile figures who spearheaded the movement, such as Sir George Lansbury, leader of the Labour Party between 1932–35, the poet Siegfried Sassoon, Labour politician Arthur Ponsonby, the Reverend Donald Soper, writer Aldous Huxley, feminist Vera Brittain and the Reverend Dick Sheppard, many of whom were involved in more than one peace organisation. There were former First World War conscientious objectors, such as Harold Bing, Herbert Runham Brown and Fenner Brockway to say nothing of the thousands of younger men and women who came into the peace movement because of what they had seen, heard or read about the horrors of war.

Some involved themselves in the movement because they came from pacifist families, while others were the sons or daughters of men who had been conscientious objectors during the First World War and were brought up to believe that war was wrong. Kathleen Wigham was born in Blackburn, Lancashire in 1919, one of eight children. Her parents were members of the Spiritualist Church and of the Independent Labour Party (ILP). They were convinced pacifists and had assisted First World War conscientious objectors: 'We were certainly against war. My mother and father wouldn't allow war toys in the home and I can remember my mother being appalled when my youngest brother exchanged one of his Christmas toys for a sort of dagger, which was harmless really because the blade part disappeared into the handle when you struck somebody, but the idea of putting your hand up to strike somebody was so abhorrent to my parents that he had go back and get his Christmas toy back.' Kathleen too became a pacifist and was involved with the Quakers. Believing that 'war is wrong and also futile because it doesn't solve the problem, it doesn't bring about the peace that we want', she gravitated to the peace movement during the 1930s. Kathleen joined the Fellowship of Reconciliation (FoR) and ultimately went to prison for making a conscientious objection against being drafted into civilian war work.

Many who became peace campaigners were horrified by what they had seen of the impact of war and were determined to do what they could to prevent another. Some had lost fathers or family members in the war or had fathers return injured or shell-shocked. Even those whose families had supported war and continued to do so found the reality of war impossible to accept. Some were drawn into the peace movement by powerful anti-war literature or inspirational speakers such as Dick Sheppard, founder of the Peace Pledge Union. Sheppard and the Reverend Donald Soper, whose speeches denouncing war were delivered in the open air at Speakers Corner, Hyde Park, or Tower Hill, made a lasting impact on those who heard them.

Born in Manchester into a 'very middle-class background', Tony Parker developed his anti-war views largely as a result of the books he read. His father ran a second-hand bookshop and many of the books in the shop: 'were from the mass of material that came out of the First World War – Siegfried Sassoon, Robert Graves, Wilfred Owen and other anti-war writers – and these affected me and I became very anti-war. It was the complete waste of life, the nonsensical way of trying to stop international problems in that way and also the tremendously sad experiences that many of these writers went through.' In 1941, and despite his father's disapproval, Tony registered as a conscientious objector.

Anti-war literature

There was an outpouring of anti-war literature during the inter-war period, much of which had a powerful impact on shaping the anti-war views of young men and women. Key works included memoirs of those who had fought in the First World War, notably Edmund Blunden's *Undertones of War* (1928) and Robert Graves's *Goodbye to All that* (1929). Other influential works included Erich Marie Remarque's poignant and powerful anti-war novel *All Quiet on the Western Front* (1929) and Aldous Huxley's anti-war polemic *Ends and Means* (1937). Two other powerful anti-war books were Beverley Nichols's *Cry Havoc!* (1933), which sold some 75,000 copies and A.A. Milne's *Peace with Honour* (1934). To the disappointment of many pacifists, Milne had completely renounced his pacifism by 1940.

Peace groups

For those who wanted to work for peace or the avoidance of war, there was a wide range of peace or anti-war groups. The Fellowship of Reconciliation (FoR) was founded in 1914 by a German Lutheran Friedrich Schultz and an English Quaker Henry Hodgkin. The FoR was a Christian pacifist organisation that supported First World War conscientious objectors, then in 1919 it became an international organisation and was active during the inter-war period, attracting Quakers, Anglicans and Methodists to its ranks.

By June 1940, the FoR had about 11,000 members, including some notable pacifists such as Donald Soper, Welshman George M.L. Davies, social worker Muriel Lester, and Alex Wood, who went on to become closely involved with the Peace Pledge Union. Doris Nicholls (neé Steynor) worked with pacifist relief organisations during the Second World War and was a member of the FoR. Interviewed by the Imperial War Museum in 1980, she remembered: 'I was working in peace shops. Very much as Oxfam and War on Want have done recently, we would hire an empty peace show and put up posters ... and we'd have leaflets ... we would sit in the shop and just talk to people, sometimes stand outside and hand out leaflets.'

Muriel McMillan (neé Smith) was another member. Born in London in 1920 into a Methodist family, she worked as a secretary before the Second World War. In about 1937, she recalled, 'a gentleman came to the church to give a talk on Christian pacifism that aroused interest. Together with a lot of other young people in the church ... we eventually formed a group who felt they were committed to Christian pacifism [and] we became members of the Fellowship of Reconciliation.' Muriel's pacifism was 'based entirely on the belief that it was the way of Christ to overcome evil with good ... we did have regular meetings ... we would go to meetings around the district and in London, all of which helped to strengthen our belief in Christian pacifism.' Stella St John, who later went to prison for her conscientious stand, also joined the FoR. A socialist and a Christian, she believed that pacifism and Christianity were inseparable: 'If I wasn't a pacifist, I wouldn't have any time for Christianity.'

A whole raft of religious pacifist organisations came into being after 1918. The Society of Friends, or Quakers, was already well known for its pacifism, which had its roots in the Peace Testimony of 1661, but individual Christian denominations also set up their own peace groups. These included the Anglican Peace Fellowship, the Methodist Peace Fellowship, the Welsh Congregational and Peace Society, which was in marked contrast to the action of churches during the First World War, most of which had effectively acted as recruiting pulpits.

The No More War Movement (NMWM) was launched in 1921. Its name clearly described its aim – no more war. The NMWM was a successor to the No-Conscription Fellowship, which had been formed to oppose conscription in 1916 and assisted First World War conscientious objectors until it disbanded in 1919. Fenner Brockway, who had been a conscientious objector during the First World War, chaired the NMWM, which included pacifism and socialism in its programme. Meeting with other conscientious objectors after the war, Brockway felt they should continue 'with an organisation which should serve the cause of peace all over the world – a No More War organisation ... we had marvellous demonstrations all over the world.' Members signed a declaration not to take part in any war, to actively work to remove the causes of war and to create a new social order based on co-operation. Based in London, it made international links and attracted some leading pacifists, among them scientist Albert Einstein, who later famously argued that if two per cent of the male population refused to fight, wars would never happen. Einstein was also involved with the War Resisters International and the Peace Pledge Union.

In 1921 a small group of war resisters formed in Bilthoven, Holland. Calling itself 'Paco' (Esperanto for 'peace') the group united pacifists in Britain, Holland, Germany and Austria. Two years later, Paco moved its headquarters to London and re-launched as the War Resisters' International (WRI). The group adopted a broken rifle as its symbol and its founding declaration stated: 'War is a crime against humanity. We are therefore determined not to support any kind of war and to strive for the removal of all causes of war.' The first secretary of the WRI was Herbert Runham Brown, a former First World War conscientious objector who, during two years in prison for his beliefs, had dreamed of uniting war resisters worldwide. From 1926 a number of leading British pacifists were elected to the chair, including Fenner Brockway, George Lansbury and Arthur Ponsonby, a remarkable man and key figure in the inter-war peace movement. In 1926, Ponsonby sent a letter to the press – the so-called Peace Letter – inviting the public to sign up for peace and pledge to refuse to support moves towards war. Within a year Ponsonby had amassed 40,000 signatories, reflecting the widespread public disillusionment with war. In 1923 an American branch of the WRI was established in the United States called the War Resisters' League and by 1939 the WRI had affiliated branches in 24 countries, although its greatest strength was in Britain and the United States. Throughout the inter-war years, the WRI held international conferences on peace and disarmament and also worked to co-ordinate moves to abolish conscription and support conscientious objectors in countries where compulsory military service existed.

Then as now, women were extremely active in the peace movement and there were some very influential organisations, including the Women's International League of Peace and Freedom (WILPF). The WILPF emerged from the Congress of Women in 1915, which had come together to try and find means of stopping the 1914–18 war. The Congress did not succeed in its aims but re-organised as WILPF, continued to work strenuously for peace and disarmament during the inter-war period, with the support of First Lady Eleanor Roosevelt. In 1932 WILPF gathered some six million signatures for a World Disarmament Petition to be presented at the World Disarmament Conference in Geneva. The petition ultimately contained about eight million signatures from women in 56 countries and was delivered to the conference in truckloads.

In Britain the Women's Co-operative Guild, a formidable and radical campaigning group of mainly working-class women increasingly adopted a strong pacifist programme. During the 1920s and 1930s Guildswomen campaigned for disarmament and lobbied local education authorities to end military training in schools. In 1933 the Women's Co-operative Guild, wanting to disassociate itself from what it saw as the increasingly militaristic nature of the annual Armistice Day ceremony, introduced the white poppy as a 'pledge to peace that war must never happen again'. It could be worn on its own or with the red poppy. At the time the white poppy was contentious and in 1937 two members of the Peace Pledge Union were sacked from their jobs for wearing it. Even so, for Armistice Day 1938 sales of white paper poppies reached a record 35,000. The Guild held pacifist services and public meetings throughout the 1930s. When war became almost inevitable, a Guildswoman wrote to the then Prime Minister Neville Chamberlain in May 1939, saying: 'I have not nurtured a son for twenty years on the principles of Christianity and good citizenship … for you or any other Government to claim him now to be a cog in the wheels of a military machine which threatens mankind with annihilation … I mean to see that he shall have the life which I thrust upon him and not the living death which you seek to offer him … if you choose to collect him, you will first have to collect me.'

In Britain there was also considerable support for the League of Nations Union (LNU), which was formed in October 1918 with the aims of promoting international peace and co-operation on the principles of the League of Nations. By 1931 the LNU had a membership of more than 400,000. Until the mid-1930s, with its emphasis on negotiation and co-operation the LNU had all-party support. It was not a pacifist organisation, yet its existence and the numbers who supported it clearly indicated that for much of the inter-war period people wanted to avoid war whether they were pacifists or not.

The Peace Pledge Union
In the mid-1930s a new peace organisation emerged that would bring thousands into the peace movement and set the agenda for anti-war activism right up to the outbreak of war. It was the Peace Pledge Union (PPU). Its founder, Canon Richard (Dick) Sheppard, vicar of St Martin-in-the-Fields, was by all accounts an extraordinarily charismatic and inspirational individual. Sheppard had served as an army chaplain in a military hospital in France during the First World War. What he saw appalled him. He believed that Christianity and war could never be compatible and became a convinced and highly active pacifist, strenuously putting the case for disarmament and protesting about the increased militarism of the Armistice Day ceremonies. In 1933 Sheppard heard about a sermon on Armistice Day preached in New York by Dr Harry Emerson Fosdick, which ended with the words: 'I renounce war for its consequences, for the lies it lives on and propagates, for the undying hate it arouses, for the dictatorships it puts in place of democracy, for the starvation that stalks after it. I renounce war, and never again, directly or indirectly, will I sanction or support another.'

Influenced by these words and against a background of growing international tension, on 16 October 1933 Sheppard wrote to what was then the *Manchester Guardian* and other newspapers, inviting 'those of my sex who have so far been silent but are of this mind [to oppose violence and war]' to 'send a postcard to me within the next fortnight to say if they are willing to be called together … to vote in support of a resolution as uncompromising as the following:- We renounce war and never again, directly or indirectly, will we support or sanction another.' Sheppard's first appeal was to men, not because he was sexist but because in his view women were already making a considerable contribution to the peace movement and he felt it was time for more men to 'throw their weight into the scales against war'. For the first day or two no postcards arrived, then there was a veritable flood, so much so that the post office complained that they should have been warned. Within days, some 2,500 postcards had arrived; within three months numbers had increased to 30,000 and within a year Sheppard had received 100,000 cards pledging support.

In 1935 the first public meeting of what was initially known as Sheppard's Peace Movement took place in a packed Albert Hall in London. Some 7,000 men attended the meeting: on the platform were Sheppard, Edmund Blunden, Siegfried Sassoon, Maud Royden, and Sheppard's friend Brigadier-General Frank Crozier, a former soldier. Sybil Morrison, chronicler of the PPU, who was imprisoned in 1940 for speaking out against the war, described this initial meeting as 'unforgettably inspiring, intensely exciting, and overwhelmingly successful'. From this meeting the new organisation emerged. It set up headquarters near Trafalgar Square in London, and adopted a number of influential people as 'sponsors'. They included essayist and playwright Laurence Housman, Aldous Huxley, George Lansbury, Siegfried Sassoon, Donald Soper, literary critic and pacifist John Middleton Murry, philosopher Bertrand Russell and illustrator and writer Arthur Wragg, whose dramatic images often featured in PPU's newspaper, *Peace News*.

Sheppard's idea was simple: those who wished to renounce war should take a pledge to do so. He believed if individuals and ultimately nations pledged to renounce and take no part in war, then peace would be assured. Given this aim, in 1936 the new organisation adopted the name Peace Pledge Union. Membership was simple: those who wanted to join only had to sign the 'peace pledge'. By 1939 well over 100,000 had done so.

'I believe the world's will to peace may yet be made effective; but this can only happen if we renounce war, not only formally, but absolutely and unconditionally.'

Dick Sheppard, *We Say 'No'* (1935)

Sheppard and many of his colleagues were Christians but the PPU was non-sectarian; it was open to men of all faiths and none. From 1936 the PPU also welcomed women as members, among them the writer Vera Brittain. Anyone could join provided he or she signed the pledge and thousands did. Denis Hayes was a PPU member and later worked with the Central Board for Conscientious Objectors (CBCO), which formed to help conscientious objectors. Speaking later about the PPU, he said: 'the thing about the PPU was that it did attempt to be a union. It was open to people of all persuasions who were prepared to be signatories of the peace pledge – it put people to an immediate choice, intimating to others that they took this view. You got all sorts of folks: people with political views, with religious views, humanitarian views and people with no views at all apart from that they regarded it as wrong to take part in warfare.'

PPU groups formed in towns and villages throughout Britain and from 1936 the PPU published a weekly newspaper *Peace News*, originally set up by the FoR. Described as 'the only weekly newspaper serving all who are working for peace', copies were sold in PPU groups, at demonstrations and on the streets. By 1936 the PPU numbered some 100,000 members, and when Sheppard wrote to the press that year inviting women to sign the peace pledge again the response was enormous.

Working for peace
Throughout the 1920s and 1930s individuals and organisations, such as the PPU campaigned for peace in many different ways, attracting new members, holding public meetings and debates, and initiating new campaigns. Looking through newspapers and journals of the time it is clear that barely a week went by without either a local or national peace group holding some sort of debate or action aimed at highlighting the wish for peace. In 1926, for instance, women in towns and villages throughout Britain marched for peace as part of a massive Women's Peacemakers' Pilgrimage, which ended in London's Hyde Park. A rare piece of Pathé news footage shows literally hundreds of women, dressed in the long coats, fur neckpieces and hats of the time, carrying placards and painted banners, processing through a seaside town, possibly Penzance. The aim of the pilgrimage was to put pressure on the British government to replace war with law; namely to settle international disputes by arbitration rather than conflict. One of the main organisers was Mrs Pethick-Lawrence, a former suffragette,

who having fought long and hard for the women's vote, was now putting her energies into campaigning for peace.

Peace organisations held international conferences on the need for disarmament, as well as international camps and events where people of different nationalities could come together in the hope of fostering friendships around the world. Youth groups were also formed, and one that was particularly popular with pacifists, and still is, was the Woodcraft Folk. Common to many pacifists, then as now, was a belief that if the young were educated in co-operative living, rather than war and militarism, this would help to build a world free of war. Many campaigners studied the writings and actions of Indian leader Mohandas Gandhi, whose use of *satyagraha* (non-violent protest) was of great interest to pacifists, and Richard Gregg, the American social philosopher, who wrote an influential book on non-violent resistance that influenced the PPU for some years. Local peace groups formed and held public meetings, distributed pamphlets and held poster parades.

Born in 1902, Kenneth Wray came from a pacifist family and two of his elder brothers had been conscientious objectors during the First World War, one of them serving more than two years in prison. A profound believer in non-violence, Kenneth had read and studied Richard Gregg. In his view, pacifism was linked 'to the Albert Schweitzer movement ... it's the sanctity of life, reverence for life ... I was always preaching about pacifism.' Kenneth qualified as an architect in London in 1925, and moved to Hastings, where, with his wife Mary, he formed the Hastings Peace Group in 1928. As he later recalled: 'We thought we'd try and form some sort of peace group ... we took the Market Hall in the Old Town and ran a meeting ... we had a very wide distribution of handbills and posters ... The meeting was a success in the end. When it started at 7.30 ... our speakers were all there, there was nobody at all in the hall, so two or three of us went out into the street and accosted people ... we finished up with about 70 ... from that we formed the Hastings Peace Group ... We ran quite a lot of public meetings from 1928–35/36 in public restaurants, took halls, we got quite well-known speakers down, had topical news talks, commentaries on international news ... we made a great impression in the town, we had many poster raids and demonstrations, beach meetings ... our main plank was disarm, disarm, disarm ... the only way of achieving peace and avoiding war.'

Among other activities, Kenneth and Mary Wray held an international peace camp in their garden, wrote letters to the press, and invited Dick Sheppard to speak: 'I think that even today it was the largest meeting that the White Rock Theatre in Hastings has ever seen. It filled the hall to overflowing. The gangways were full, the back was full, the large vestibule was full and people were standing on the steps down to the street.'

Mechanisms for peace

Wanting to prevent wars was one thing; finding the means to do it was another. The immediate post-war years were optimistic. The First World War came to a formal end with the Versailles Treaty of 1919. The treaty, which Germany described as a diktat (dictated peace), fixed the blame for the war on Germany and her allies and imposed harsh reparations. Germany also had to disarm. Some people were prescient enough to realise that these harsh penalties might well lead to further conflict. However, for many years most hoped that the League of Nations, which was set up under the treaty as an international peacekeeping organisation, would provide the machinery for preventing future wars, so that the First World War would truly be the 'war to end war'.

In 1925 Britain, France, Italy, Belgium and Germany signed the Locarno Treaty, which confirmed Germany's borders with France and Belgium as inviolable and the Rhineland as a demilitarised zone. On 1 December 1925, *The Times* described it as a 'great achievement' and stated that it 'eliminates the risk of international war in a historical area of conflict for a long time to come'. Three years later, 15 nations, including France, Germany, Britain, the USA, Italy and Japan signed the Kellog-Briand Pact, which renounced war as 'an instrument of national policy', except in matters of self-defence. Ultimately 65 nations signed the pact.

Events like these seemed to sound a positive note and were perceived as major landmarks for peace, but none of them renounced war completely, nor was disarmament mentioned. As events turned out, hopes for these measures were wildly over-optimistic. In an interview for the Imperial War Museum, Donald Soper recalled: 'After the First World War, there were a good many people who thought, 'This is the end of war. We've learnt our lesson.' ... one took hope in the League of Nations and in the increased awareness of the terrible effects of war and that unless we put it behind us, it would overwhelm us ... of course, gradually the situation developed in which that high hope became an idle dream.'

Pacifist MPs

On the national stage, as far as British political parties went, views on war and militarism varied. At the end of the First World War there was a cross-party wish for peace, although no one party was strictly pacifist, apart from the Independent Labour Party (ILP). The Labour Party, however, contained a number of pacifists, some of whom had been conscientious objectors during the First World War. They included: George Lansbury MP, an outspoken pacifist and leader of the Labour Party from 1932–35; Herbert Dunnico; Arthur Ponsonby, who was Under Secretary of State for Foreign Affairs in the 1934 Labour government; and Alfred Salter.

In 1933 the Labour Party reinforced its commitment to peace at its annual conference when it passed a motion put by Sir Charles Trevelyan committing the Labour movement 'to take no part in war and resist it with [its] whole force' and to resolving international tensions through law rather than war. However, by 1934 the Labour Party was shifting ground and moving towards an acceptance of the need for war, on the grounds of 'collective security' in the face of an aggressor. George Lansbury resigned the following year and towards the end of 1936 pacifist MPs formed themselves into a Parliamentary Pacifist Group. This included MPs such as James Barr, George Hardie, George Lansbury, Henry McGhee, Fred Messer, Alfred Salter, Reginald Sorenson and Cecil Wilson, as well as a number of peers, like Arnold Sydney, Gavin Faringdon, Arthur Ponsonby and Henry Sanderson.

Cracks appear

As time went on, however, it became increasingly clear that the world was not yet ready for peace and by the 1930s the international situation was showing worrying signs of unrest. In Italy, Benito Mussolini had adopted Fascism, an extreme right-wing nationalist political programme. By 1923, as Il Duce, Mussolini had become dictator of Italy, dismantling democratic structures and imposing a one-party Fascist state. In 1935 Italian troops invaded what was then known as Abyssinia (now Ethiopia) and incorporated it into Mussolini's new

Italian Empire. The League of Nations completely failed to prevent this act of aggression. Unfortunately this was not the first time that the League had failed to live up to its expectations. In 1931 Japan had invaded Manchuria and, although China called on the League for help, Japan refused to leave Manchuria and instead left the League.

More worrying though was the rise of the extreme right-wing nationalistic National Socialist (Nazi) party in Germany, under the leadership of Adolf Hitler, a self-declared anti-Semite, who was determined to restore Germany's greatness following the punitive terms of the Treaty of Versailles. In 1933 Hitler took control of the German state as Chancellor and set about dismantling democratic structures. Then from 1935, he embarked on an extensive re-armament programme and introduced conscription. The League failed to respond to any of the violations of international treaties and in March 1936 Hitler ordered his troops to re-occupy the Rhineland, which had been a de-militarised zone since 1919. In October 1936 Hitler signed the Rome-Berlin Axis with Mussolini and in November agreed to an Anti-Comintern Pact with Japan. By 1937 Germany, Italy and Japan had withdrawn from the League of Nations: it was becoming increasingly clear that the world was heading for war again.

Events such as these dented the optimism of the peace movement. Hopes for even limited disarmament were further dashed when a long-planned World Disarmament Conference held in Geneva from 1932–4, failed to reach an agreement. From 1936 escalating conflicts tested the peace movement. Revolution and civil war broke out in Spain, causing divisions among pacifists, with many wanting to support the Spanish Republicans against Franco's Nationalist forces. Some individuals gave up their pacifism and went to Spain to fight and even those who did not felt that Spain challenged their pacifist consciences. Clifford Simmons, a pacifist and social worker, who was active in the PPU wrote later: 'if there were ever any justification for war the struggle of the Spanish people against the forces of Fascism was surely it. However, believing that one should not take life in any circumstances and that violence would beget violence, I could only stand miserably aside and watch the departure of some of my friends.' When the Second World War began Clifford registered as a conscientious objector but subsequently changed his mind.

The Spanish Civil War was hotly debated in the pages of *Peace News*. Many could understand why people who considered themselves pacifists might want to fight for the Spanish cause. The PPU, however, maintained its pacifist stand, believing as George Lansbury wrote in *Peace News* on 29 August 1936, 'Those who condemn human slaughter must do so at all times.' To many people's surprise though, Fenner Brockway, who had been an absolutist conscientious objector during the First World War renounced his pacifism at this point, feeling that while he would never consider shooting anyone and would continue active in the peace movement, 'politically and realistically' he could no longer justify the absolutist pacifist position.

False hope

In Britain it seemed that pacifism still held sway when in February 1933, ten days after Hitler came to power, the Oxford University Union debated the motion that 'This House will in no circumstances fight for King and Country'. The motion was presented by Dr Cyril Joad, a skilled orator and a high-profile campaigner in the peace movement, and was carried by 275 votes to 153 against. The press highlighted the result and there was something of an outcry. Winston Churchill was particularly disgusted, describing it as a 'very disquieting and disgusting symptom', presumably of a spineless, unpatriotic youth. There were even suggestions that the debate might have helped to persuade Hitler that Britain would be unwilling to go to war. Tony Parker, who later registered as a conscientious objector, said he was often told that the Oxford Union debate had caused the war: 'One had the image of Hitler reading this in the morning paper and saying "Right, now is the time for me to strike at England".' In actual fact there is no evidence that the debate or indeed any pacifist activity played any part in Hitler's war plans nor, as events turned out, did the debate stop most young men from accepting conscription when the time came. What it possibly demonstrated was that highly jingoistic appeals to young recruits would not work again.

In 1934 the LNU organised a nationwide ballot, popularly known as the Peace Ballot, to find out what the British public thought of war, disarmament and the League of Nations. Volunteers trudged from house to house delivering ballot sheets and there were irascible letters in local papers complaining about the waste of time and money but more than eleven and a half million people voted, answering a series of five questions. The results were revealing. More than 90 per cent favoured economic and non-military measures of countering an attack, which pacifists saw as a victory. However, the survey also showed that 70 per cent would support military measures should Britain be attacked. As the *Birmingham Post* pointed out: 'the answers given are most significant … peace-loving as this nation is, it still believes in a resort to arms.' Even while the ballot was being carried out, Mussolini had launched his invasion of Abyssinia, and in Germany Hitler was cementing his power base.

Campaigning steps up

As war came closer, the PPU, which merged with the NMWM in 1937, and other peace groups stepped up their campaigning. One of the most high profile campaigns came from the PPU's decision not to co-operate with the British government's air raid precaution practice drills on the grounds that 'the organisation of anti-gas drill with "blackouts" and sham air raids cannot fail to produce in the public mind a despairing expectation of war as inevitable' (*Peace News*, 23 January 1937). Actions took place across the country with peace activists demonstrating against moves to war, disrupting ARP presentations and staging counter demonstrations when mock air raids took place. Activists also leafleted against war and held poster parades, which angered some members of the public. A Mr Harry Montana from Brighton, for instance, wrote to *The Times* protesting about a PPU leaflet criticising the ARP, storming angrily: 'public opinion should be aroused generally against an insignificant minority of the misguided, responsible for circulating such dangerous rubbish.' By and large the public was tolerant of anti-war campaigners, but even so in Walthamstow peace activists were ordered to remove an anti-ARP poster and the Chief Constable of Penzance sent PPU leaflets to the Home Office asking whether they constituted a 'public nuisance'. In May 1938 pacifist posters outside the Curzon Cinema in London were torn down. Despite such expressions of hostility, local groups in places such as Reading and Eccles opened peace shops, displayed anti-war and pacifist literature and engaged the public in debate.

Sheppard died suddenly in 1937, which was a terrible blow for the peace movement, but, as he had said, the movement was bigger than he was, and activists continued to work for peace. In April 1938 the PPU and WRI launched a manifesto presenting a constructive alternative to war, on the basis that saying 'no' to war was not enough. It was sent to the British prime minister and secretary of state, as well as to the ambassadors of Germany, Italy, France, the USA, Japan, China and the Soviet Union, and called for the need to meet 'the economic requirements of the large masses of poverty-stricken people'. The manifesto had virtually no impact and the move towards war now seemed almost inevitable. The Munich Agreement of 30 September 1938, which allowed Nazi Germany to annexe the Sudetenland area of Czechoslovakia, briefly appeared to halt outright war. Many pacifists felt it came at a terrible cost, namely the dividing up of Czechoslovakia by Nazi Germany, even if the full invasion did not happen until 1939. In October 1938 a deputation of leading pacifists, including Vera Brittain, George Lansbury, Sir Alfred Salter and Laurence Housman went to Downing Street to urge the setting up of a global peace conference. By March 1939 more than one million people in Britain had signed a peace petition calling for such a conference. Realistically though, it was much too late.

Munich was merely a breathing space and one that upset many pacifists. There were accusations that members of the peace movement and the PPU in particular were pro-Nazi, which is rather like accusing all communists of supporting Stalin. It could not have been further from the truth: pacifists and peace activists were just as appalled by the anti-Semitism and totalitarianism of Nazi Germany as anyone else, but they did not believe that killing and war was the way to resolve the situation. On the eve of war, the peace movement in Britain still numbered many tens of thousands. The PPU alone had a membership of well over 100,000. But being a pacifist in peacetime was one thing; refusing to fight or to participate in the war effort once war began might not be so easy. As war became increasingly likely, men and women had to search their consciences and decide what stand they would take if and when war broke out. It was the introduction of conscription that would force many people to decide.

Chapter 2

Conscription and War

'Making the choice to be a conscientious objector was simpler once war came.'

Eric Farley

Despite considerable protests, conscription, or compulsory military service, was first introduced into Britain in 1916 when, with men dying by the thousands in the trenches, the British Army desperately needed more soldiers. Three years later, with the war over, conscription was dispensed with, so that during the inter-war period entry into the army was voluntary, unlike many other countries. However, by the mid-1930s with the international situation deteriorating and a second global conflict on the horizon, the possibility of conscription being re-introduced was being discussed. From 1935 successive governments stated that conscription would not be re-introduced during peacetime. In a pre-election speech on 13 November 1935 Stanley Baldwin denied a rumour that there were plans to do this and on 1 April 1936, when Baldwin, now prime minister, was asked by an MP for a guarantee that conscription would not be re-introduced during peacetime, he replied, 'Yes, Sir, so far as the present Government are concerned.' Rumours continued to circulate and in January 1937 Duff Cooper, Secretary of State for War, in a lunchtime speech at the Constitutional Club, stated that he had 'never contemplated conscription in peace time'. Again, on 17 February 1938, Neville Chamberlain, who had now replaced Baldwin as prime minister, pledged in the House of Commons not to bring in peacetime conscription. For the general public, this was a relief: Britain was re-arming, but while there was no conscription, people still hoped there would be no war.

The peace movement was less sanguine. As early as 1936, Britain's allies, particularly France, were putting pressure on the British government to re-introduce conscription. Following a clumsy statement by Sir Thomas Inskip in the House of Commons in May 1938, it was revealed that plans for re-introducing conscription did exist, but at that time the prime minister stated clearly that they did not intend to carry them out. Naturally pacifists were opposed to conscription: writing to *The Times* on 1 May 1939 Henry Carter, Charles Raven and others expressed the view that 'the compulsory training of men to slaughter their fellow-men is to us intolerable,' while 'socially too, conscription is a retrograde step, a move away from democracy towards the enthronement of militarism and totalitarianism.' Pacifists also argued if conscription were re-introduced during peacetime it would, like ARP manoeuvres, send the message that war was inevitable.

In fact quite a number of people opposed conscription and not all of them were pacifists by any means. There were many who felt the imposition of conscription was a totalitarian measure quite unsuited to the democratic nature of British society. Military historian Liddell Hart, for instance, stated in a letter to *The Times* on 24 March 1939 that to introduce compulsory service would be 'a definite surrender of our own vital principles,' arguing that it would be a 'decisive step towards totalitarianism.' The trade union movement too was opposed to conscription, not just military but also industrial conscription, on the basis that it would give the state too much control over working men and could mean an end to the labour movement.

Given this situation, the Government and other organisations focused initially on encouraging voluntary recruitment into the armed forces. In January 1939 the Citizen Service League, formerly the Army and Home Empire Defence League, was launched with the aim of training 'the youth of the country to fit them to be of use in times of national emergency'. At around the same time, the Government urged recruitment through national service. Some 200 National Service Committees were established where voluntary recruits could sign up and the Government produced a 48-page booklet, the *National Service Appeal Handbook,* which was dropped through the letterbox of every household in Britain. The booklet spelled out ways in which the British people could start preparing for war, and listed various fields of service.

According to *Peace News*, this was conscription by the back door – persuasion rather than compulsion – and in response the PPU produced its own *Peace Service Handbook*, which it described as 'a guide suggesting some of ways in which the people of Britain can help their country and the world to live at peace.' The PPU's resources did not allow for blanket distribution but some 200,000 copies were printed and distributed for sale through various PPU groups around the country. Unfortunately the handbook backfired rather badly; at the end of the pamphlet the PPU listed a number of international friendship organisations, one of which turned out to be a front for Nazi sympathisers. The PPU came in for criticism and accusations of being pro-Nazi, although nothing could have been further from the truth – their 'crime' was to have been naïve. In the event the PPU withdrew the handbook.

Nevertheless, it was increasingly clear that conscription was coming. In January 1939 the peace movement made a last ditch attempt to prevent it and launched the No-Conscription League. Writing in *Peace News*, Runham Brown, one of the PPU's sponsors and former conscientious objector, explained that he had joined the No-Conscription League 'because the policy of preparing for war by drawing everyone into its service, first by persuasion then by deception and propaganda and finally by open compulsion is a policy which will bring war.' He went on to state that he loathed war 'because it brings untold suffering and ruin but most of all because it destroys all that is best in man. As a young man I refused to fight; now as an older one I am more than ever determined to resist an effort to persuade, to cudgel, and at last by open compulsion, to drive the younger generation to take part in that thing which destroys both body and soul.'

Conscription returns
The PPU was swimming against the tide. War was approaching and in April 1939 the government, having gained trade union approval, announced plans to introduce compulsory military training for young men. There was opposition from pacifist MPs in the House, but the Military Training Bill, which introduced 'a limited and temporary measure of compulsory military training', became law on 26 May 1939. Under the Act, which was intended to last for three years, young men aged 20 and 21 were obliged to register at their local office of the

Ministry of Labour. They would then be liable to be called up for six months training, usually in the army but in a few instances in the Royal Navy or Air Force. Following training, they would be transferred into the Reserve. It was estimated this would affect some 310,000 young men.

The Military Training Act was Britain's first ever act of peacetime conscription, but only one registration took place. On Saturday 3 June 1939, 240,757 young men were registered at employment exchanges throughout the country. The first conscripts were called up on 1 July 1939, but escalating events soon made the Act redundant. On 1 September 1939 Germany invaded Poland; two days later, Britain and the Empire and France declared war on Germany. World War Two had begun; that same day a whole raft of wartime regulations were passed into law, including the National Service (Armed Forces) Act, which allowed for conscription of men aged 18 to 41. The upper age limit was raised to 51 in December 1941.

Just a few days before the Military Training Bill had passed the House of Commons, the PPU together with the Women's Co-operative Guild and various peace and youth groups organised an anti-conscription demonstration in London's West End. According to a report in *The Times*, some 5,000 men and women took part and the demonstration stretched for a mile. It was also stated that nearly 1,000 conscientious objectors under the age of 25 were involved. By and large though the National Service Act passed with little public protest, probably because by this time there was not much point in wasting energies. War had arrived and so had conscription. For those who had been active in the peace movement, this was effectively 'make up your mind time' – were the thousands of men who had been involved in the peace movement going to accept military service and pick up arms, or not?

The 'conscience clause'
In fact men had the legal right to refuse conscription on grounds of conscience. Both the Military Training Act and the National Service (Armed Forces) Act contained what was known as the 'conscience clause,' whereby men liable for conscription could apply for exemption on grounds of conscience. Once provisionally registered, a conscientious objector then appeared before a tribunal which assessed the applicant's sincerity and decided whether the objector would be exempted or not.

'If any person liable under this Act to be called up for service claims that he conscientiously objects —

to being registered in the military service register, or

to performing military service, or

to performing combatant duties,

he may, on furnishing the prescribed particulars about himself, apply in the prescribed manner to be registered as a conscientious objector.'

Like conscription itself, the 'conscience clause' recognising the rights of conscientious objectors was not new. It had been included in the Military Services Act of 1916, but the official attitude towards conscientious objectors during the First World War was almost entirely brutal and punitive. Tribunals, which were under the aegis of the War Office, rarely showed any sympathy for the conscientious objectors who appeared before them and every effort was made to get men off the register of conscientious objectors and into the armed forces, members of the tribunals often seeing themselves as recruiting agents.

The official attitude during the Second World War was completely different. During the second reading of the Military Training Bill on 4 May 1939 – the same day that the no-conscription demonstration took place in London – Chamberlain, who had himself served on the Birmingham Tribunal during the First World War, told the House of Commons that there was 'one class of exemption which is of particular importance and which is the subject of special treatment ... that of the Conscientious Objectors, who are provided for in Clause 3.' Chamberlain acknowledged that this was a class of people who 'must necessarily always present great difficulties.' Yet he went on to say, 'We all recognize that there are people who have perfectly genuine and very deep-seated scruples on the subject of military service, and even if we do not agree with these scruples at any rate we can respect them if they are honestly held.' He hoped that the Act dealt with them in a 'broad-minded manner' and also commented that, based on the experiences of the First World War it was 'both a useless and exasperating waste of time and effort to attempt to force such people to act in a manner which was contrary to their principles,' (*The Times*, 5 May 1939).

There were various reasons for this more tolerant attitude. No doubt as Chamberlain indicated, the courage of conscientious objectors during the First World War was a major factor. Many of them had endured long and repeated prison sentences; some were taken to France and sentenced to death. The death sentences were not carried out but the unshakeable determination of First World War conscientious objectors to stick to their principles no matter what pressures were put on them created a lasting impression. The fact also that they had existed in the First World War meant they were already familiar and it was assumed they would exist again in the Second. In addition if, as was said, Britain was fighting a totalitarian regime in the name of democracy and freedom, it would be a massive contradiction to persecute individuals for expressing their deeply held convictions. Either way, the official treatment of conscientious objectors during the Second World War was definitely more humane, as some who had been objectors 20 years earlier, such as Harold Bing, recognised: 'The National Services Acts were more generously drafted, the tribunals were more carefully appointed and there was no military representative on them ... the hearings were all, I think, much fairer.'

It is possible also that the British government had no wish to create martyrs this time around, as Denis Hayes, who worked with the Central Board for Conscientious Objectors during the war, believed: 'it stemmed from the fact that they did not want to make martyrs. They'd had martyrs in 1916–18 and they found it was counter-productive ... those people who were perhaps lined up before a firing squad, only to be told they would have to come back another day. They were getting relatively good publicity ... they didn't want that to happen.' There were exceptions, particularly after 1940 when France fell to Nazi Germany, and attitudes towards pacifists and conscientious objectors, which had been tolerant, hardened. Quite a few conscientious objectors during the Second World War experienced hardship, hostility and discrimination. Many were victimised, some went to prison, and many lost their jobs. There were also instances of brutality.

Conscripting women

From 1941 women were also conscripted but their situation was rather different from that of men. The National Service (No. 2) Act, which was introduced in December 1941, mobilised single women aged 20–31, who did not have children. Although women were not allowed to engage in combat, under this Act they had the same right of conscientious objection as men. If a woman registered as a CO, she would be offered alternative civilian work, such as farming or work in hospitals. If she also refused this work, then she had to appear before a local tribunal. The Registration for Employment Orders was introduced in April 1941 and under this all women aged 19–40 had to register at their local employment exchange and could be directed into work of national importance, such as nursing, munitions, factory or other work. It was effectively industrial conscription and did not carry the same legal right of conscientious objection.

Make-up-your-mind time

Clearly pacifists in Britain had hoped and worked hard for peace throughout the inter-war years, and therefore the arrival of war, after years of trying to prevent it, was depressing. David Spreckley, an anarchist and active PPU member until 1941, listened to Neville Chamberlain's speech in the PPU offices: 'I remember standing there with tears flowing down my face ... because we'd failed, a total feeling of failure, thinking "My God, we've tried, and we've tried and we've failed".' For Joan Pasco, who was active with the PPU in Slough: 'We were as active as possible ... one lives on a hope that it [war] won't happen. It was such a terrible period.' Following the announcement of war, PPU members walked in silence from Dick Sheppard House to Hyde Park, where they held a silent vigil.

While the majority of the country faced the outbreak of war with resignation and apprehension, for pacifists the arrival of war and conscription meant that pacifism was no longer just a theoretical position. Now they had to decide what action they were going to take, and for men of call-up age, this meant whether they would refuse to be conscripted. For some it was not an easy decision. Tom Haley, a printer's apprentice in London, was 18 when the war started: 'I knew my call-up was imminent: was I going to join the armed forces or sign on as a conscientious objector? Despite all my feelings against war, the decision was not an easy one to take. But this was make-up-your-mind time.' Tom Haley did register as a conscientious objector and worked with the Friends Ambulance Unit (FAU) during the war.

Many pacifists had thought long and hard about what they were going to do if or when war arrived and some expressed their concerns publicly. On 19 May 1939 *Peace News* featured an article by Rose Macaulay entitled 'The Pacifist Dilemma', in which she said: 'Faced on one side with a regime more brutal than any we have had in Europe since Alva and his Spanish torturers ... on the other with a horrible and inhuman war (which our Government would not wage to save the Czechs), what is the pacifist to feel or do? What attitude is possible that is neither callous, bellicose nor silly?' She concluded: 'It is no doubt because I am not a good pacifist that I cannot answer my own question.'

Rose Macaulay abandoned her pacifism in the face of Nazism, as did several others, including Cyril Joad, Bertrand Russell, Maud Royden and the writer Storm Jameson, each of whom had been extremely active in the peace movement. Other public figures who retreated from their pacifism included the writer A.A. Milne. Having written *Peace with Honour* in 1935, which Denis Hayes described as 'one of the finest expositions of the pacifist case,' Milne completely reversed his position in *War with Honour*, published in 1940. He not only gave 'Hitlerism' as his reason, but also in a poem beginning 'Your Conscience is "against" the war?' wrote scathingly against the conscientious objector. Even Beverley Nichols, who had declared he would be a conscientious objector in the next war, moved away from his pacifism when the war began.

Despite those who stepped back from their pacifism, many did not renounce their anti-war position, although sticking to this in the face of Nazism was not always easy and could involve some soul-searching. William Elliot, a clergyman who registered as a conscientious objector, had grown up in an Anglican family and became a pacifist when he was still at school, refusing to join the Officers Training Corps (OTC), despite considerable opposition from his headmaster. In 1926 he joined the No More War Movement (NMWM) and he signed the peace pledge when the PPU was formed. William said later: 'I think the signing of the card meant commitment ... of course there was a terrific falling away when the war began. People who had signed in a great moment of emotion and quite sincerely ... were moved in the other direction and for that matter who wasn't? I had terrific wrestles with my conscience going on all the time, right on during the war. I remember one night I walked about all night instead of going to bed when there had been a particularly dastardly raid on our shores by the Nazis and then, of course, commonsense prevailed and I realised we were doing exactly the same thing to them. This was the crux of the whole thing. Retaliation was no good. But certainly it wasn't without terrific heart-searching.'

Another who thought hard about his decision was Eric Farley. Born in 1919, he was a committed socialist and humanist. He was about 20 when the Military Training Act was introduced and knew that he would probably need to register in September 1939. In his unpublished memoirs, *A Partial View*, Eric described how he: 'felt trapped by the prospect. Fortunately the brave pioneers of the 1914–18 war had established the possibility of conscientious objection to military service and this right was recognised by a clause in the Act of 1939. So there was a choice, though not an easy one. Without going deeply into cause and effect, it was quite evident that, for the opposition and the Jews, gypsies and other inconvenient minorities Nazi Germany was an indescribably horrifying place to live in. This situation had ... been ignored by the governments of Europe until Hitler's expansionist aims were confirmed as totally serious by his actions, and became a threat to the other countries' markets ... there was a convincing argument that Hitler must be stopped and that the only way was by military force. On the other hand it seemed to me that the endless chain of military murder being countered only by greater murder had to be stopped.

'I was greatly influenced by Tolstoy's *War and Peace* and Aldous Huxley's *Ends and Means*. I thought of myself positively as a pacifist and not simply a negative conscientious objector. Pacifism ... provided an alternative means of action, though I was not at all sure that, if put to the test, I should be brave enough or charitable enough. How would it be possible to love Hitler or Himmler and not want them dead. But few human situations and dilemmas are subject to simple solutions. My simplification, pacifism, at least did not require me to kill one human being. It was in favour of life.' Observing that when war came, 'the very great majority of people opted for the other simplification, military force as regrettably the only way of stopping Hitler', Eric

Farley chose to register as a conscientious objector, saying that 'paradoxically making the choice to be a conscientious objector was simpler once war came than it had been in peacetime.' Some had no doubts about the action they would take. After their years of working for peace, Kenneth and Mary Wray knew exactly what they would do; 'we were both determined to honour the pledge of Sheppard as closely as we could.'

In 1939 the PPU had a membership of somewhere between 100,000 to 130,000, but not all PPU members became conscientious objectors during the war. According to Sybil Morrison, Dick Sheppard had said that if war came he believed that about 50 per cent of the signatories to the pledge would change their minds and he was about right. Actor Paul Eddington, a pacifist who registered as a conscientious objector believed that: 'the moment the war happened the vast majority of people who had professed themselves to be pacifists said, "Well, fundamentally I am a pacifist, but now this situation is with us we've got to do something about it." It's a position I can understand, but it did reveal their pacifism to be not very deep-rooted.'

It was a view shared, somewhat more dismissively, by David Spreckley, who described the majority of PPU members as 'deadweight ... who just signed their postcards and then sat on them.' This is probably unfair: no doubt thousands of people genuinely believed that they were pacifists during the inter-war years but once war began, and with the threat from Hitler, they renounced their position. It took courage and a deeply held conviction to make the choice to become a conscientious objector in the face of Nazism and Fascism and as much as possible individual choice was respected. Writing in *Peace News* on 14 April 1939, Arthur Wragg had stated: 'It is important in this coming year for all members to realize where they stand in regard to their pledge. The whole basis of the PPU is freedom of conscience to do what individuals feel to be right ... We must not allow ourselves to impose our own feelings on the consciences of others.' Impressively this respect for individual conscience was a constantly recurring theme within the peace movement as war approached, and among most conscientious objectors once war arrived. Despite those who dropped out, when conscription was introduced thousands of men and women stuck to their beliefs and went on to take their stand as conscientious objectors and they did so in far greater numbers than in the First World War.

Who were the conscientious objectors?

During the First World War, some 16,000 men registered as conscientious objectors. In the Second World War more than 62,600 men registered as conscientious objectors between October 1939 and June 1945, not counting the 4,900 or so who registered as objectors under the Military Training Act. About 1,000 women registered as conscientious objectors. So, who were the conscientious objectors (COs), or 'conchies' as they were often disparagingly known? And as the pioneering social research organisation Mass Observation, which carried out an investigation into pacifism and conscientious objection, asked: what gave them 'the courage and determination' to persist in their views?

For a start there was no such thing as a 'typical' conscientious objector. They included a remarkable range of highly individual men and women who had a wide variety of beliefs, occupations and backgrounds. They were artists, musicians, civil servants, shipping clerks, social workers, local government employees, shop workers, teachers, electricians, carpenters, journalists, solicitors, bricklayers, lay preachers and students. Some were, or became, very well known in their field. They included the actor Paul Edington, musician and entertainer Donald Swann, and Sydney Carter, who composed 'Lord of the Dance'. Composer Michael Tippett, who was imprisoned in 1943, was a conscientious objector, as were playwright Christopher Fry, Oliver Postgate, creator of the much-loved children's television programme *The Clangers* and George Lee, who in 1957 became the first general secretary of Mencap. The crystallographer Kathleen Lonsdale, who spent a month in Holloway Prison for refusing compulsory fire-watching duties, was a conscientious objector, as was Joyce Allen, who on 2 April 1942 became the first woman conscientious objector to appear before a tribunal.

Others included: Tony Parker; Kathleen Wigham, who trained as a teacher for children with special needs; Angela Sinclair-Loutit, whose father had fought in the First World War; Brian Phillips, a Quaker, whose father had been a CO; and not forgetting the many thousands of others. They were all quite different individuals. As Denis Hayes described in his book *Challenge of Conscience*: 'C.O.s were of entirely divergent types, ranging from the Plymouth Brethren and the Jehovah's Witnesses who took little part in the affairs of the world to the extreme Socialists and anti-parliamentary Communists … from the philosophical anarchists to the Roman Catholics, with most denominations and movements ... finding a place between these two extremes ... They were neither saints nor sinners, but ordinary likeable men and women.'

The one thing they had in common, and what made them conscientious objectors, was that they all refused, on grounds of conscience, to be conscripted for military service or, (in the case of women from 1941), refused to be conscripted for certain types of civilian service. But even then many took their stand for different reasons. Sometimes their views were formed as a result of growing up in a pacifist family, the children of pacifists often became conscientious objectors; others had been influenced by what they had read or teachings they had encountered. Many had deeply held religious convictions; others had moral objections to war and killing; and still others arrived at their stand for political or humanitarian reasons. Personal and political reasons caused Reginald Bottini to become a conscientious objector. Born in 1916 into a family of Italian restaurant workers who had arrived in Tooting in the early 1900s, Reginald was an only child whose father had been killed in France during the First World War when he was not much more than a year old: 'My mother was widowed at the age of 23, my father having died on active service in France ... I remember my mother sobbing quite often when I was a child.' Bottini became a socialist and active member of the Balham and Tooting Labour Party, where he became known as an 'anti-war socialist.' He said in an interview with the Imperial War Museum that he never 'adopted the pacifist stand' because he thought that in certain circumstances violence was inevitable but when war arrived, he took a conscientious stand against it. He spent the war years working on the land and after the war became active in the National Union of Agricultural Workers.

As well as differences in background, COs also had contrasting views on the degree to which they were prepared to participate or not in the war machine. Some took an absolutist stand and were not willing to be involved in any aspect of the war; others were prepared to do some sort of civilian work, particularly if it had a humanitarian aspect, provided it was under civilian control and did not run counter to their conscience; and still others anticipated doing non-combatant duties in the military. Each individual conscientious objector made his or her own decision about where they drew their line, according to their conscience. Joan Pasco was born in 1913, the daughter of a socialist. A socialist and pacifist herself, she was active with the PPU in Slough before the war. She felt that when war began: 'People were put to the test. There were degrees of pacifism: there were those who would go into the medical service because they were helping to save people and not to kill them. There were those who would take alternative service such as work on the land … and there were those who wouldn't do anything, they would just go to prison and try not to be part of the war machine at all although the criticism was … that they were eating the food the ships managed to bring in … It was a very difficult situation. I feel it's up to everybody to examine their own conscience and see where you come to the dividing line.'

'Odd and arty'
Mass Observation carried out an extremely detailed study of pacifism and conscientious objection as one of its many surveys into British daily life during the Second World War. The material was collated into a 100-page report entitled *Conscientious Objection and Pacifism 1939–1944* and sits in boxes at Sussex University and makes fascinating reading. Mass Observation volunteers attended meetings of the PPU and other peace groups, talked to people in the street, interviewed conscientious objectors, attended registration and tribunal days and carried out surveys on the class, age, background, occupations and motivations of conscientious objectors, as well as looking at public attitudes. According to their findings, conscientious objectors tended to belong 'largely to the middle and lower-middle classes'. They came from all over the British Isles although most came from London and the South East. On registration day 21 October 1939, for instance, more than eight per cent of those registering as conscientious objectors came from London and South East. Norwich was also mentioned as a strong centre for pacifism, probably because Max Plowman and John Middleton Murry lived nearby. According to a report in *The Times* (19 June 1940), 40 per cent of Norwich City Council employees had registered as conscientious objectors. A large number also came from Wales, where Methodism and Welsh nationalism have shaped a long tradition of pacifism.

Amusingly, the Mass Observation writers stated that 'to the conventionally minded some of them look odd and arty ... Actually the chief odd things from the conventional point of view are a tendency to be vegetarian, love their mothers, love animals, and not all of these things are unconventional.' As it happens, many conscientious objectors were vegetarian, a choice closely linked to their refusal to kill and they included a number of artists but 'odd' is not really the right word, although many people thought so. They were individualistic, but also highly principled and thoughtful people who believed that on grounds of conscience they would not be conscripted.

Differing views

Men and women of all religious faiths and of none became conscientious objectors. There were Anglicans, Methodists, Christadelphians, Jehovah's Witnesses, Baptists – and not surprisingly Quakers. Brian Phillips, whom I was fortunate enough to interview for this book, registered as a CO in 1942 and came from a well-established Quaker family. His father, Charles, had been a conscientious objector during the First World War and his brothers, Merlin and Geoffrey, as well as his brother-in-law Peter Shea, also registered as conscientious objectors during the Second World War. For Brian, as for so many Quakers, pacifism was 'one of the deep roots of Quakerism' and becoming a conscientious objector was almost a foregone conclusion.

Despite the preponderance of religious conscientious objectors, there were others who had no religious faith and arrived at their stand through their political views, including socialists such as Tony Parker and Eric Farley. Some combined Christianity and socialism; there were also anarchists and those who took a humanitarian or moral stand. Peter Sharp, a conscientious objector who was directed to work on the land by his tribunal stated in an interview with the Imperial War Museum: 'It was a surprise to me how many reasons there were for being war-refusers. To start with there were the spiritualists, whom we referred to as the "crazy gang"; they were mostly odd and didn't seem to have any idea of pacifism or anything else. Then there were the Christadelphians ... There were straight anarchists, some who had been Communists ... We came from very mixed backgrounds, professionals and artisans.'

Nor were all conscientious objectors pacifists; the two were not synonymous. Some who registered as conscientious objectors, particularly socialists, had fought in the Spanish Civil War during the 1930s but were not prepared to take part in the Second World War. Jehovah's Witnesses also were not pacifists. Douglas Beavor, an absolutist conscientious objector imprisoned during the war, was interviewed by the Imperial War Museum in 1980: 'I would not call myself a pacifist, the war of Armageddon I would support, although not by bearing arms or taking part, but I would be in complete agreement with it.' It was a view that both tribunals and conscientious · objectors often found difficult to understand.

Quite a number had already been very active in the peace or anti-war movement before the war, which stood them in good stead when it came to appearing before their local tribunal. But not all had done so. Fred Vahey, for instance, was very much a loner. Although he wrote regularly to *Peace News* and had taken the peace pledge, he never attended meetings; according to his daughter Lorna, he was not someone who joined groups. Born into an impoverished family in Ireland, his mother had been in domestic service, and he saw first-hand, not just the war wounded of the First World War, but also how working people were exploited. According to Lorna this was a great influence on his pacifist views: 'it wasn't totally the influence of war … a big thing was being brought up by servants, on big estates … everything seemed to relate to the idea that people with power have power over other people. It always seemed as if his politics were formed pretty early from those experiences of life as a servant and the First World War and then unemployment … I was always quite impressed … he never even went to secondary school … how he tried to sort out how the world worked … I think it was this whole corrupt society, which was based on power and greed and manipulation of ordinary working people.' Fred was impressed by Henry George, the American political economist who argued for the common ownership of land, and was determined to live a life that exploited neither humans nor land, which played a large part in his decision to be a conscientious objector. However, no matter how much conscientious objectors differed in their backgrounds, views and motivations, the first step towards becoming a conscientious objector was registration.

International situation

Very few countries made provision for conscientious objectors during the Second World War. The United States was one of the minority that did. The Selective Training and Service Act was passed on 16 September 1940, before America entered the war. It called for the drafting of able-bodied men aged 19 to 44 and included a section – 5(g) – explaining how a man could obtain exemption as a conscientious objector. Exemption was allowed on grounds of 'reason of religious training and belief'. Objectors appeared before a Selective Service board and if found genuine would most usually be directed into work of 'national importance' under civilian control.

Australia, New Zealand and Canada also made provision for COs, although unconditional exemption was not provided for; instead objectors were directed into civilian service. Of the three, only Australia recognised non-religious objectors: under the Defence Act, September 1939, a man's conscientious objection did not have to be 'of a religious character' or 'part of the doctrine of any religion'. Instead a man's sincerity was the key issue, rather than his motivating belief. There were about 11,000 conscientious objectors in Canada; just under 3,000 in New Zealand and about 2,700 in Australia. Elsewhere, those who openly declared a conscientious objection to war risked at best imprisonment and at worst execution. This applied in Austria, Belgium, Bulgaria, Czechoslovakia, Finland, France, Germany, Hungary, Italy, Norway, Poland, Portugal, Spain, Russia and Yugoslavia. Denmark operated an alternative service for COs, even under Nazi occupation and there was some provision in Norway and Sweden. The USSR had some provision for COs, but it ended in 1939.

The regime in Nazi Germany ruthlessly suppressed pacifist activity both in Germany and in Nazi-occupied territories during the war. The penalties for expressing conscientious objection were very harsh. A number of Roman Catholic conscientious objectors were executed, among them Franz Jagerstatter, an Austrian who was openly anti-Nazi and declared publicly that he would not fight. He was conscripted, declared his conscientious objection, only to be imprisoned and later executed.

Chapter 3

Taking a Stand: Registration

'It felt as though you were separating yourself from the rest of the world.'
Edward Blishen

Under the 1939 National Service Act, all eligible men aged 18 to 41 had to register at their local employment exchange for service in one of the armed forces. Conscientious objectors also had to register, but they applied to be put on a special register. Not only was registration the first step for a conscientious objector, but it was also often the first time a man publicly declared his intention to be a conscientious objector. Although they had the legal right to do so, some found the process a bit daunting. Even though William Elliot had been a pacifist since his schooldays, he found the idea of registering as a CO more intimidating than the tribunal that would follow. His wife was also a pacifist and Elliot asked her: '"What would you think of me if I come back and tell you I haven't registered as a conscientious objector?" "My goodness, I'd be ashamed of you," she said, and of course that gave me what I needed and I went to the chap and said "I want to register as a conscientious objector," and quite contrary to what I thought would happen … I thought I might be subject to a whole string of abuse … he said "Oh well, if you would just go and wait over there, while I deal with these other fellows; we have to fill in a different form." And having passed that hurdle, I didn't find [the tribunal] so difficult.'

Despite William Elliot's anxieties, there was little abuse from staff at the employment exchanges or from the men who were signing up for military service. Mass Observation volunteers observed registration days at some 40 different labour exchanges and only overheard four deliberately aggressive comments from staff. By and large, staff at the exchanges, no matter what their personal opinions might have been, treated conscientious objectors in a reasonably professional or matter of fact manner, although there were exceptions.

All men entered the same building but once inside COs were told to go to separate counters or through different doors to register. It was not always clear what they were supposed to do or where they were expected to go. There was rarely any guidance and some conscientious objectors felt slightly bemused. Objectors registering at Waltham Green, for instance, were highly amused to find information chalked on a blackboard telling them that they needed to register at the 'girls' entrance'.

Registration was by age group and always took place on Saturdays. There were 39 registrations during the war. Men aged 20–23 were registered in 1939 and those aged 23–35 were registered in 1940. By mid-1941 all men aged 20–41 had been registered. After 1941, men aged 19 registered, followed by men aged 18. From 1939–45 a total of 8,355,500 men were registered, including those registered under the Military Training Act. Of these, 6,700 registered as conscientious objectors. The percentage of COs was very small and was highest at the start of the war. On registration day 21 October 1939, 2.2 per cent of men registering were conscientious objectors. On 6 July 1940, just after the fall of France, this had dropped to 0.57 per cent.

Feeling different

Many objectors were reasonably confident when they arrived to register; some were slightly defensive and others were quite nervous. One who found the experience unsettling was Len Richardson. An insurance clerk and a Christadelphian, he was deeply convinced that Christ's teachings required him to refuse to take up arms, but he felt very uncomfortable lining up to register as a conscientious objector with other young men of his own age: 'on the morning … when I had to declare my conscience before men, I was far from feeling cocky about it all … I hardly dare glance round for fear of seeing any of my old friends from the local grammar school, with whom I had previously been one of the boys on the Rugby football field.' However when Len's turn came, he said he wanted to be registered as a Christadelphian conscientious objector.

Feeling different or isolated from one's peers was a common experience for conscientious objectors, yet it went with the territory. As the whole country was put onto a war footing, particularly after France fell to Nazi Germany in June 1940, COs were by definition operating outside the mainstream and many of them felt their difference quite acutely when they went to register. Author and broadcaster Edward Blishen said it took 'a lot of courage'. Blishen was born in 1920; his father had fought in the trenches during the First World War and had returned home wounded and suffering from shell shock. He was not sympathetic to pacifists. However, influenced by his father's experiences and by the anti-war literature he had read, Edward Blishen knew he could not take part in killing and decided to register as a conscientious objector. 'You had to register yourself in the local post office and everybody was declaring themselves at a certain counter, and there was this forlorn counter over here in order to declare that you were not going to join in … it felt as though you were separating yourself from the rest of the world … It wasn't a pleasant thing … it did require courage … the courage of separating yourself from your friends … and a feeling that the whole flood of emotion was opposed to what you intended to do … But … I was absolutely determined not to be drawn in.'

As the vast majority of men signed up for military service, the pressure to conform was considerable. Eric Farley later described how some of his friends tried to persuade him to change his mind: 'On the day my group was to be called up I went to the Wimbledon Labour Exchange to register provisionally as a conscientious objector … Many of my friends and acquaintances were also there registering for one form or other of military service. They tried to persuade me not to take such an opposite and damaging course. One in particular put the point that many felt the same way but that now it had come the war could not be stopped by the few like me. Why not then accept the inevitable? In any case the majority of people even in the services wouldn't actually be called upon to fight and we might hope to be employed in a non-combatant capacity. This particular friend indeed had his wish come true. He spent the war years in the safety and comfort of Ilfracombe, in the Royal Army Pay Corps. But I had made up my mind and went my solitary way to a little-used counter to register provisionally as a conscientious objector.' At about the same time, feeling the need 'to be with people of like views,' Eric Farley joined the Wimbledon Group of the Peace Pledge Union (PPU).

One conscientious objector who, temporarily, found the emotional and social pressure too great was Walter Wright. He was a civil servant and profoundly opposed to war but in 1940, one week before he was due to register, he began to have 'serious doubts' as to whether he would be doing the right thing by registering as a conscientious objector, given that so many of his friends were being called up. Increasingly, despite his anti-war views, Walter began to feel that he would be letting down his friends and his country so that when the day came he registered for military service. Soon after, however, and realising that he had gone against his true beliefs, he re-registered as a conscientious objector.

Shock and disgust

From 1941 women too had to register at employment exchanges. Though women were not allowed to engage in combat, they could be directed into one of the women's services – the Army Territorial Service (ATS), Women's Auxiliary Air Force (WAAF) or Women's Royal Naval Service (WRNS) – or into civilian work such as the Women's Land Army, munitions factories or civil defence, which also became compulsory at that time. Women too, approached the business of registering as conscientious objectors with mixed feelings. Ifanwy Williams, who spoke to me about her experiences for this book, had studied to be a social worker at Liverpool University. She went to Wrexham to register. Her brother, Glyn Roberts, an architect, was also a conscientious objector and influenced by him and books such as Huxley's *Ends and Means*, Ifanwy was determined not to do anything to help the war effort. Her mother disagreed fiercely with her pacifism, but nevertheless Ifanwy registered as a conscientious objector and remembered 'the look of shock and horror and the disgust' of people standing behind her when she announced her position at the employment exchange. Probably because Ifanwy was doing social work, there was no follow up and she did not have to appear in front of a tribunal. She continued to work as a social worker, qualifying in 1943, and also met with other pacifists and conscientious objectors during the war, selling copies of *Peace News* in the streets.

After the war she remained an active member of the Fellowship of Reconciliation.

As a convinced pacifist, Kathleen Wigham also registered as a conscientious objector. She encountered a fairly hostile reaction: 'When I went to register, this gentleman came and spoke to me. I said, "I've come to register as a conscientious objector because I object to doing any work which will relieve anyone else to military service." He said, "Oh, you're one of those, are you, we didn't expect women coming along." I said, "Well, I may be the first but there will be more to follow." So he took various particulars and dropped some casual remarks about being a coward and not being able to see straight, and told me, "Well, you'll be hearing from us".'

Muriel Macmillan registered as a conscientious objector and in an interview with the Imperial War Museum said that she felt women did not get the same sort of attention as men. She believed that: 'girls in those days weren't taken all that much notice of as conscientious objectors, it was the men who were really much more involved, girls of course did not have to register at first, in fact I think the first registration was in 1941, when the 20–21 age groups had to register, they were usually I think given the opportunity of joining one of the three forces or doing alternative work in munitions, the Land Army, or the fire service. I registered as a conscientious objector and would have been quite prepared to do nursing or Land Army, anything under civilian control other than munitions but in fact my firm reserved the few girls who were in it. I was asked by the secretary if I wished to be reserved when I registered as I told him I was a conscientious objector and I said I had no objection to being reserved if that what was what he intended anyway, but I did not at all wish to be treated differently because I had been registered as a CO.'

Personal statements

Although the procedure was fairly straightforward, *Peace News* provided weekly advice for those who were going to register as conscientious objectors. The paper outlined the terms of the National Service Act and advised potential objectors to say immediately that they intended to register as a conscientious objector when they arrived at their local employment exchange, before answering any questions or filling in any forms. Applicants were usually, though not always, taken into a separate room and asked to provide personal details – name, address, parents, occupation and marital status. These details were recorded and the objector was provisionally placed on the register of conscientious objectors and given a certificate of registration. They were also given another form to take away. This was where the applicant wrote his personal statement outlining and explaining the reasons for conscientious objection. It had to be completed and returned to the Ministry of Labour and National Service within 14 days of registering. On a section at the back of the form the applicant was instructed to indicate precisely what they objected to, namely: '(a) to being registered in the Military Service Register; (b) to performing military service; (c) to performing combatant duties.' Applicants were told to strike out the options that did not apply to them. Many COs did not strike out any of the options, but explained in their personal statements whether they were looking for absolute exemption, whether they would do civilian work or participate in the war effort in some way that did not conflict with their consciences, even to the extent of undertaking non-combatant duties. Others expressed specific preferences, such as working with the Friends Ambulance Service.

Personal statements were as individual as the objectors themselves, reflecting the beliefs of the objector, whether religious, political, humanitarian or moral or a combination of all. Some statements were short, blunt and to the point. Frederick Morel registered as a conscientious objector in 1940. A political objector, his statement, dated 15 August 1940 stated: 'As a member of the working class it has been my firm conviction for the past sixteen years that war does not solve any of the difficulties of the countries of the world, but only increases the poverty, degradation and misery of the working classes. I cannot therefore take life in defence of a system which serves only a minority of the peoples of the world and which, while it remains it can hold no future for the common people. Since leaving school I have devoted my time to the interest of my fellow man the world over. I therefore wish to claim total exemption from Military service.' Morel's local tribunal was not satisfied with this and dismissed his application.

Ron Huzzard, a socialist and peace campaigner, also presented a fairly short statement, which incorporated his religious beliefs: 'As war is incompatible with Christianity and my pacifist beliefs and contrary to all the ideals that I strive to live up to, I cannot but refuse to undergo military service of any kind or condone the waging of the current conflict. I am convinced that it is basically wrong to attempt to destroy evil by evil means and that the wrongs of the world today can only be cured by applying the law of love and goodwill towards all and overcoming evil with good. In this I sincerely believe and after my sixteen years in the Christian Church I know that it is my duty to obey the voice of my conscience rather than the call of the state.' Ron appeared before his local tribunal in Leeds on 20 March 1940. His application was dismissed on the grounds that the tribunal doubted his sincerity because 'fundamentally his objection is political'.

Religion was a powerful motivating force for many objectors, who profoundly believed that there was no place for war and militarism within their spiritual beliefs and their statements outlined this stand. Charles Hope Gill, who registered as a CO in 1943, wrote in his statement that 'all war is not only contrary but definitely opposed to the teaching of Christ ... Christ taught us to say "Our Father" thereby implying that all men are brothers, without distinction of race or colour, and as one who is trying to follow Him, I cannot therefore take any part in the mass murder and torture of my fellow men.'

Some statements were extremely detailed, providing information about family upbringing, schooling, links to churches and/or pacifist organisations and occupation. Many also explained the process by which they had arrived at the decision to make a conscientious objection. Whatever their length or detail, it was the personal statements, together with questions about an applicant's views, that tribunals used when assessing the sincerity of an applicant.

Fred Vahey's personal statement (1940)

'I refuse to be conscripted because it is a denial of human liberty. I claim, as an individual, the right to act towards my fellow individuals, and no less to all creation, in the manner that my intelligence and my convictions guide me through the medium of my conscience. Whatever may be the reason for the Universe, I see it was a whole – composed of subsidiary parts and each part is again made of small units – infinitive.

'The perfection of the whole is dependant on the wholeness of its component parts. The human race is dependent on its individuals and each individual is, consciously or unconsciously, part of the whole and his actions should be such that he hinders not, nor exploits, nor harms in any way other individuals. His duty to his neighbour is obviously to do unto him as he would like to be done unto. If he acts contrary to this he will be told so by his conscience. A man may exploit, or even kill his neighbour and drown his conscience in patriotic hysteria or some other anodyne, but mankind does not end at national frontiers, so to kill a neighbour for patriotic reasons is a crime against humanity and can only be done for the material gain it may give to a special section, and to conscript individuals for patriotic adventure is especially criminal and should not be tolerated. A man's conscience is his most precious possession, and if the state within whose boundaries he resides attempts to conscript him into armies, organised and ordered to do to his neighbours in other states, things he would be punished for doing to his neighbours within his own state, and things that he can have no desire to be done to himself, then he must resist.

'Exploitation is one of the basic crimes of human society and conscription is one of its crudest forms. Our whole "capitalistic" civilisation is built on exploitation. Right at the foundation where the land, from which all men must obtain their needs, is in the hands of a few, thus throwing the masses of men onto the labour market where they are exploited by their more privileged brothers. Exploitation increases as the power of privilege grows over the disinherited. The state, the mouthpiece of privilege, becomes a tyrant backed by the armed forces it has set up for the maintaining and furthering of privilege and exploitation – empires etc. But exploitation goes even beyond the boundaries of human persons.

'... Some fourteen years ago I realised that the exploitation of anything was immoral and since then I have lived as a vegetarian. Later, from the same motive, I abandoned the "capitalistic" way of life and have lived now for some few years on a small plot of land, growing my simple food, and following my principles of non-exploitation of brother men, animals, nor soil, and endeavouring to meet animosity, where encountered, with friendliness. To follow this path, with humanity at large pursuing other goals, means abandoning material comforts often, but the wholeness of conscience is worth preserving, and this I mean to do, war or peace, conscription or democracy, and the state and all its material power may whistle.'

Refusing to register

Some conscientious objectors refused to comply with the process of conscription at all and did not register, believing that to do so was to co-operate with a system with which they profoundly disagreed. One was Reginald Porcas, who worked for the local government in Croydon. Reginald was also a pacifist and active in the PPU. His was an interesting case. Events began on 3 June 1939 at the time of the Military Training Act, when Reginald wrote to the Minister of Labour, Ernest Brown, saying that although he knew young men aged 20–21 needed to register for military training, or apply to go on a special register of conscientious objectors, he had no intention of doing so. Reginald explained: 'as a conscientious objector, I cannot admit to the moral right or competence of any tribunal to pass judgement upon my claim or conscience.' He also stated that he was registering 'my strongest protest to the principle of conscription in any form. Conscription implies a training for the murder of my fellow beings, and it is my intention to resist that to the limit of my strength.'

A few days later Porcas received a polite letter from Croydon employment exchange, inviting him to come and see them. Another letter, dated 26 June 1939, was sent to Porcas enclosing a leaflet explaining the terms of the Military Training Act, pointing out that the Act catered for conscientious objectors, explaining that there was a specific procedure for 'safeguarding the position of persons who have genuine objections on grounds of conscience', and that Porcas's original letter did not in itself provide evidence that he was a conscience objector. Porcas replied that he was 'fully conversant' with the terms of the Military Training Act but emphasised that he could not reconcile himself to the 'rightness of submitting the sincerity of my hatred of learning to kill my fellow creatures to any tribunal no matter how constituted'. He also stated that he did not acknowledge the 'moral right or competence' of a tribunal to judge conscience, repeating his unalterable decision not to register, 'no matter what action you decide to take against me'.

Following more letters, in July Porcas agreed to see a Mr Ince, a high-up official from the Ministry of Labour, who visited Porcas at his house in an attempt to encourage him to register, as this was the law. In August, Porcas wrote again to Ernest Brown, Minister of Labour, pointing out that well before the interview, he had taken a 'lively interest' in the Military Training Act and understood very well its provisions and possible penalties if he refused to register. Nevertheless, he was not going to do so, even if this was illegal. He did not recognise the ability of any tribunal to judge his conscience.

Various letters passed between the Ministry of Labour and Porcas, one of which warned him that he would be fined if he continued to refuse to register until, finally, in November by which time Britain was at war, Porcas received a letter telling him that he had been provisionally registered as a conscientious objector, under the provisions of the National Service Act, which empowered the Ministry of Labour to register a man as a conscientious objector, even if he refused to register. On 10 November he received an application form for his tribunal hearing.

Reginald Porcas was clearly not delighted and refused to attend his tribunal. In his letter to the tribunal, which was held in Fulham Town Hall, he stated: 'It is because I believe in human freedom and the respect for the human personality, that I refuse to appear before a tribunal. I regard it as disgraceful that in England, in the twentieth century, individuals should be arraigned before a tribunal to be examined as to whether they hold a conscientious objection to the soul destroying filth of militarism, to the mass murder of their brethren, and to the compulsory inculcation of bestiality and inhumanity into young men. Brought up to believe that murder was the gravest of all crimes, to believe in the sanctity of human life, and to respect human personality, I cannot bring myself to change these beliefs, to condone wholesale slaughter ... The war method has been tried countless times, and has always failed miserably ... That war brings out the best in man is a lie; it merely harnesses the best in man to the vilest and most immoral of all purposes, the violent and cruel destruction of mankind. This ... should be sufficient to make all decent people affirm their resolve to have nothing to do with it, to refuse to take part in the slaughter and to spend their lives working for the creation of a world in which the war method has been made impossible, a world wherein we may live at peace with each other ... Such a world will come into being when men renounce the war method by refusing to fight.'

On 12 December 1939 the tribunal went ahead without Reginald. His letters were used as evidence but because he was not there and could not answer questions, the tribunal argued they could not judge his sincerity, and took his name off the CO register and placed him on the military register. Surprisingly the Ministry of Labour appealed against the decision. They argued that there were 'reasonable grounds' for thinking that Porcas was a genuine conscientious objector, that the local tribunal should have dealt with the case using the evidence before them, and that on that evidence Porcas should be given unconditional exemption. An appeal was arranged and Porcas was notified but again, thanking the Ministry for the trouble they were taking and not wishing to be disrespectful, said on grounds of conscience he would not attend. Soon afterwards, he was informed that he needed to attend a medical examination prior to be being conscripted into the army. He refused.

In February 1940 the appeal tribunal took place with a Mr Henderson representing the Minister for Labour and arguing for the local tribunal's decision to be overturned. Porcas's letters were used as evidence. Still uncertain, the appellate tribunal adjourned. The Ministry of Labour wrote to Porcas asking him to provide references; Porcas agreed on the condition that his references confirmed he was a pacifist but did not argue his case. Two of his friends provided testimonials confirming his sincerity, trustworthiness and the fact that he was an active member of the PPU, and in July 1940, more than a year after he had refused to register, the appellate tribunal decided that Porcas should 'without conditions be registered in the Register of Conscientious Objectors'. He was given unconditional exemption. He was though dismissed from his job.

Reginald Porcas's case was interesting and unusual, like that of a second conscientious objector Horace Mayo, who also refused to register. It demonstrated how far a determined and principled man would take his conscientious stand, no matter what the consequences. It also showed that there were people in the Ministry of Labour who appeared to want to be as fair as possible. The case caused something of a stir, and what Denis Hayes described as a 'lively discussion' took place in the House of Commons on 25 July 1940. It began when Colonel Burton and Ernest Thurtle both asked Ernest Bevin how the situation had come about. Mr Thurtle even suggested that Bevin's Department by deliberately supporting the men, who had refused to recognise the Military Training Act, 'was in fact supporting contempt for the law,' an accusation that Bevin completely dismissed. Either way the situation did not arise again: in future if conscientious objectors were not prepared to apply to a local tribunal, their cases would be heard in their absence and they would have to abide by the decisions.

Other conscientious objectors also refused on much the same grounds but not necessarily with the same consequences. Kenneth and Mary Wray, who had campaigned strenuously for peace right up to the outbreak of war refused to register when war arrived: 'we were both determined to honour the pledge of Sheppard as closely as we could … We neither of us registered, we neither of us registered for anything at any time.' On each occasion when he should have registered, he wrote to the authorities and told them, 'on no account was I going to register … and they could do what they liked. They always wrote back of course and said you are subject to dire penalties if you don't.' Wray even wrote to Bevin telling him. 'I made it very clear nothing on earth would shift me and nothing happened, much to my annoyance … I felt that somehow I must bear witness to what I believe and I would like it known that the witness is there … just from the point of propaganda.'

In the event, rather to Wray's annoyance, nothing happened: Wray was not called up nor was he penalised in anyway. Describing himself as a 'willing martyr' he was not sure why there were no repercussions. Perhaps it was because he was such a well known peace personality in the locality but maybe it also was because the government, as Denis Hayes believed, had learned from experiences during the First World War and had determined not to make martyrs of conscientious objectors. Either way, Wray later said that the government was extraordinarily tolerant. While he had been robbed of the chance to publicise his stand, he nevertheless thought it 'was a very great thing to have a government who would take that attitude, "well, we can do nothing with this man, we'll leave him alone".'

Other objectors too refused to register on grounds of principle. Like many other pacifists Tom Carlile, an anarchist from London's East End, had been fiercely opposed to Hitler and Nazism since the early 1930s but did not consider that killing other human beings was any way to counteract them. He opposed conscription because he felt the state had no right to tell him who to fight and kill and refused to register. Tom wrote to the Ministry telling them and was provisionally registered as a CO. Tom's tribunal hearing took place in his absence and his case was dismissed. Denis Allen also did not register: 'I took the view that if I registered and took exemption in the normal way, I was subscribing to the pattern of war.' He acknowledged that the government was 'enlightened' in providing this opportunity and acknowledged that his situation would have been very different in

Nazi Germany, but 'that didn't alter the fundamental principle, so I wrote and said I wasn't going to register'.

Advice and support
Those whose principles would not allow them to register were a minority. By far the greatest numbers went through the registration process. Many COs received support from friends and family – William Elliott, Kenneth Wray and Fred Vahey for instance were fortunate to be married to women who were also pacifists and supported their actions, or took a conscientious stand themselves. Others such as Brian Phillips were the sons or daughters of First World War objectors, with first-hand experience of the situation and its difficulties. Muriel McMillan too came from a pacifist family and her then fiancé Arthur McMillan was a conscientious objector. But others did not have the same support; instead their stand was met with disapproval and could put a considerable strain on personal relationships, adding to the sense of isolation and of being an outsider that many COs experienced. Tony Parker had a girlfriend with whom he was very deeply involved. One evening she said to him, '"My father says if you don't give up this attitude, I'm not to see you again". I said, "How do you feel about that?" and she said, "I have to do what my father says." She was only 18. I said, "I'm sorry, I'm not going to change my attitude," and I never saw her again but I've often thought back … how strange it had been because I would probably have been married to her now if I hadn't been a conchy.'

Various organisations gave support to COs. Chief among these was the Central Board for Conscientious Objectors (CBCO), formed in 1939 to provide help and support for conscientious objectors on every matter from registration through to preparing for tribunals. The CBCO co-ordinated various pacifist groups, kept a watchful eye on all legislation relating to conscription, lobbied parliament when necessary, and attended tribunals and appeals. As well as providing advice and monitoring legislation, the CBCO also kept detailed records, many of which are now in the archives of the Peace Pledge Union and the Quaker Library in London. It also set up an employment agency to help COs who because of prejudice might find it difficult to obtain employment and provided practical help to families of COs suffering as a result of their stand.

The CBCO was not a campaigning organisation; it existed to protect the rights of conscientious objectors. Fenner Brockway, although no longer a pacifist, was its chairman, a position he accepted because: 'I believe in freedom of conscience so much ... I believe so deeply in personal liberty and if anyone felt within themselves that they could not fight, even if I thought the war was just, I recognised that they had a right to their conscientious objection and I remained the chairman ... all through the war.' Its officers included Denis Hayes, who described the work of the CBCO in his book *Challenge of Conscience* (1949). Born in 1915, Hayes came from a 'typical middle-class background'. One of his earliest recollections was being held aloft to watch 'a triumphal procession of the forces on their return from service'. Even at that age, he felt it was 'a waste of time going'.

Denis started developing his pacifism in his late teens: 'I'd considered seriously two alternatives: one was that of collective security, where I'd read some of Sir Norman Angell and other writers ... on the other hand there was some publicity being given to the pacifist view partly through the writings and preaching of Dick Sheppard.' Influenced also by A.A. Milne's book on pacifism, Beverley Nichols, and Donald Soper ('a rip roaring pacifist') whom he heard speak at Kingsway Hall in London, he signed the peace pledge and when war arrived registered as a conscientious objector. His prepared statement consisted of 'more or less quotations. I didn't say anything particularly personal ... I was taking the unconditionalist stand.' He was granted total exemption. 'I was then serving as an assistant solicitor. My principal whom I'd been articled to felt that in view of my personal beliefs ... it would be preferable for me not to remain on the staff and he gave me the opportunity of resigning, which I did ... after that I was asked if I would go to the Central Board and take charge of their publications.' The CBCO had its headquarters in London, sharing a building with the PPU, but also had regional and local branches. Hayes, who had been a local and regional secretary with the CBCO, had studied the legal situation of COs and 'was keen to do what I could ... my training and attitude had coincided and I was able to help other folks.' His main job was to look after the Board's publications, but he also used 'to keep an eye on the changes in the law [and] write accounts of legal position of COs arising from the changes'. He also edited the CBCO journal, *Bulletin*, which 'was difficult because of paper rationing but we got a small allocation of paper from the government'.

The CBCO helped any conscientious objector who approached them, whether a pacifist or not and its attention to detail, its specialist knowledge and fair-mindedness won it the support of government and others. But COs were its primary concern. As Fenner Brockway said in his foreword to Denis Hayes's book, 'legislative, administrative and informative services were the bricks and mortar of the work of the Board. Its heart was human sympathy and help for the individual C.O. and his or her family.'

The PPU too provided help and support for conscientious objectors, although it sometimes got into trouble as a result. Occasionally PPU members waited outside employment exchanges on registration days offering leaflets to men who were going in to register as conscientious objectors. Within no time at all the press seized on this and accused the PPU of picketing and attempting to change the minds of men who were bent on registering for the military. The issue was even raised in the House of Commons. On 23 February 1940 *The Times* reported that Sir W. Davison MP had asked the Home Secretary whether he was aware of the 'subversive activities of a body known as the Peace Pledge Union', who were 'picketing employment exchanges and endeavouring to induce men to join their organisation'. Sir J. Anderson, the Home Secretary, reassured the questioner that the activities 'of this organisation' were being 'carefully watched'. The explanation though was far more innocent; concerned that nervous conscientious objectors might not be certain of their rights, members of the PPU were on hand with leaflets to reassure them, and as they publicly stated in *Peace News*, there was no subversive intent at all. However, it was neither the first nor the last time that the PPU came under surveillance.

'Shirkers'?

At the time, and even since the war, there were people who believed conscientious objectors were just 'shirkers', trying to get out of military service by whatever means possible. In his statement to the House of Commons about provisions for conscientious objectors in May 1939, Chamberlain had made a reference to 'shirkers', saying 'there are those, very few in number ... who are really shirkers, and who would take advantage of exemptions of this kind to avoid a duty which lies upon every citizen.' However this was very far off the mark. Perhaps there were a few, but as pacifist Joan Pasco commented, 'there were very, very, very few conscientious objectors just dodging military service; there easier ways of dodging than to go in front of a tribunal'.

Perhaps more significantly there were COs who registered even though they did not need to. In some cases they were in 'reserved' occupations, such as teaching, or were too old for conscription, but still felt that they could not take what they saw as the easy way out, so instead determined to bear witness and take a stand. Ernest Lenderyou worked in a pharmaceutical research laboratory, which was one of the reserved occupations and would not have been called up. 'Working in a pharmaceutical research laboratory … I would have found difficulty in being accepted for service in the armed forces even as a volunteer. But in view of my firm opposition to the war and the war machine, that in turn had come to seem like a 'cop-out'. He therefore registered as a CO.

Joyce Allen was working as a teacher when conscription for women came in. She could easily have asked for exemption, but like many others registered as a CO as a matter of principle, though when she appeared at her tribunal she was told to continue teaching. Another who registered as a matter of principle was Leonard Bird, who could have avoided conscription because he was a student and because the firm that employed him wanted to keep him. Leonard was subsequently imprisoned for refusing alternative civilian work.

Chapter 4

Taking a Stand: Tribunals

'If you object to taking life, why aren't you a vegetarian?'
Tribunal question put to conscientious objectors

Having registered as a conscientious objector, an applicant waited to
be called to appear before a local tribunal. There were 12 regional
tribunals in England and Wales and four in Scotland. The regional
tribunals were held in county courts in towns and cities such as
Glasgow, Leeds, London, Newcastle, Manchester and Southampton.
Tribunal panels consisted of what Denis Hayes, CBCO officer,
described as 'five wise men', namely a chairman and four others. In
England and Wales the chairman was a county court judge and in
Scotland a sheriff fulfilled the role. The other four members of the
panel, who were usually professional men, had to include a trade
unionist and a woman if a female applicant was appearing. Pacifist and
former leader of the Labour Party George Lansbury had hoped panel
members would be young, but in practice their average age was
around 65. This meant that most tribunal members were at least twice
the age of the young applicants appearing in front of them, many of
whom were in their twenties.

The job of the local tribunals was to assess an objector's sincerity and
to decide whether objectors should be exempted from military service
or not. Tribunals had existed during the First World War, but were
then under the aegis of the War Office and rarely showed any
sympathy for the conscientious objectors who appeared before them.
Every effort was made to get them into the armed forces, tribunal
members, many of whom were military personnel, often seeing
themselves as recruiting agents. One major change during the Second

World War was that the Ministry of Labour and National Service rather than the War Office administered the conscientious objectors' tribunals and those who served on the tribunals were chosen carefully; there were no military representatives. According to Denis Hayes: 'the tribunals were quite nice folk on the whole. You didn't have a military representative which was the bane of the First World War; they were all rather carefully selected. You had an academic, you had a county court chairman … you had someone appointed after consultation with the trade unions.' Generally, too, tribunal members were more sympathetic or at least more understanding of conscientious objectors because of the First World War pioneers. There were many instances of harassment and bullying and times when personal prejudice was obvious but by and large tribunals attempted to be as reasonable as possible. If a conscientious objector considered that the tribunal's decision was unacceptable, he or she could go to appeal at special appellate tribunals.

Preparing for a tribunal

Applicants received written notification of their tribunal dates and venues, usually with plenty of notice. The waiting period between registration and a tribunal hearing varied: at the beginning of the war, tribunals were overloaded and applicants had to wait several months for a hearing. By 1941 the number of applicants had declined and the waiting period was much shorter. While waiting to be called, applicants carried on with their normal lives as best they could and prepared for the coming tribunal. Some attended mock tribunals, which were organised by groups like the CBCO. Participants, who included veteran conscientious objectors from the First World War, role-played tribunal panels, levelling questions at an applicant to prepare them for the real life experience. Some conscientious objectors thought this was cheating; others, like Eric Farley, found it useful although outcomes were not always accurate. Eric was active with his local Peace Pledge Union group in Wimbledon: 'An increasingly important function was an advisory service for C.O.s at local level … For those approaching their first hearing mock tribunals were held whose rulings tended to be favourable. For example, I was granted exemption which was the opposite of what happened when I appeared in January 1940 to state my case before the tribunal in Great Portland Street.'

The CBCO, PPU and other organisations produced pamphlets with advice and examples of questions that COs might face. One pamphlet, *The London Tribunal Questions the CO*, published by the London Friends' Local Conscription Committee in 1939, was for men due to appear before the London tribunals. It listed questions under various headings: preliminary, general, religious and political and included questions such as: 'Are you sure that your objection is one of conscience and not of reasoning or mere dislike?'; 'Why would you not be willing to defend other people's happiness and freedom?'; 'Do you not think the soldiers are standing up for what they think right?' 'If you love your fellow men do you not want to protect them?'; 'If you object to taking life, are you a vegetarian?'; What would you do if other people, or children, were attacked in your presence?'; and 'Why is it wrong to defend your country in time of danger?'. While no doubt the questions were intended to be searching or probing, they were in practice often seen by COs are either extremely idiotic or highly provocative.

Groups helping conscientious objectors strongly advised against learning answers by rote. Another pamphlet *The CO and the Tribunal*, was published by the Joint Advisory Bureau, an umbrella group that represented many anti-conscription groups. It organised sample questions thematically and included points to consider when formulating an answer. It was not a crib but a thoughtful exploration of issues that might arise and how a conscientious objector might want to respond; its aim was to help the applicant clarify his thinking. Some tribunal judges accused pacifist organisations of coaching objectors but support organisations emphasised the need for objectors to know their own minds. As the introduction to *The CO and the Tribunal* stated: 'Many applicants have asked for specimen answers to questions. These are not provided. They might be too exactly repeated at tribunals, which would do the applicants no good. They might also lead applicants to take up attitudes which they were not capable of sustaining under examination.'

Tribunal procedure

Objectors could be accompanied by friends and family, and were encouraged to bring witnesses to their tribunals. Angela Sinclair-Loutit for instance brought her father, who had been a general in the First World War; others brought colleagues from peace organisations or members of their church who were prepared to provide evidence of an applicant's sincerity. Hearings were also open to the public and the press, which could be a double-edged sword. The press highlighted anything they considered to be dramatic and local newspapers usually reported on members of the community who were appearing in front of tribunals, which could be embarrassing. One individual who fell foul of the press was student Cecil Davies who, thinking he was promoting 'the cause', allowed himself to be photographed by the *Daily Express*. The results were horrendous; his photograph, which presented him as a rather languid youth, appeared in the paper under the provocative heading 'Conchie No. 1' and a quote 'I won't fight, I won't do A.R.P. work'. The accompanying article painted Davies in a biased and malign fashion, which led to some very abusive letters arriving through his letter box: 'Somebody had cut out the photograph, wiped their bottom on it, and sent it off in an envelope. Not very pleasant.' Davies considered he had been 'conned' and very 'naïve'; the paper had taken him to a pub and plied him with drink, resulting in a very slanted interview.

Tribunal procedure itself was fairly straightforward. Hearings were often held in county courts or council chambers: the panel sat at one table and the objector was at another, or even in a dock, together with any witnesses and papers. The objector was handed a copy of his personal statement, which the panel also had. Sometimes it was read out, or just referred to, then the panel cross-examined the objector about his or her background, occupation, activities and beliefs in an attempt to assess the applicant's sincerity. Once the questioning was over, the panel considered their decision, which could be done in private but often happened in the court. Hearings usually lasted between 10–20 minutes although some were so rushed that conscientious objectors were given no time to explain themselves.

In February 1940, *The Tribunal*, the journal of the Fellowship of Conscientious Objectors, included a piece by Rev. D.R. Mace, who had accompanied a young objector to an appeal tribunal: 'He was told to arrive at the court at 4 p.m. on the day of his hearing. I went with him as a witness. He was not called until 5.20 when nearly everyone had left. The members of the Tribunal had obviously had a long, tiring day. They were no doubt weary, ready for a meal. The room was very stuffy. They asked him a few questions about his job and his home circumstances. I was then given the opportunity to speak for him. I explained the circumstances ... sat down and waited for the cross-examination to begin. *It never did begin.* After a brief whispered consultation, the Chairman announced that the Tribunal found no evidence of a conscientious objection in his statement and saw no reason to alter the decision of the Regional Tribunal. It was all over ... this young man had been judged without ever being heard; judged on a written statement in which he declared participation to war to be contrary to the principles he held sacred in the name of humanity. If an objection based on principles held sacred is not conscientious, I felt I would have to start looking for a new meaning of the word "conscience".'

Undignified and unseemly

Local tribunals were tasked with the job of assessing the sincerity of the conscientious objectors, although as more than one objector asked: how can you test the sincerity of a person's conscience? It was an impossible task, not made any easier by the fact that the National Service Acts did not define 'conscience'. Some tribunal chairmen sought guidance but most arrived at their own definitions, which led to quite a degree of variation in the way tribunals handled cases. Tribunal members were expected to be impartial – Judge Burgis of the North-Western Tribunal had said their role was not to determine whether applicants' views were 'reasonable or patriotic' but whether they were 'sincerely and deeply held' – and to leave any personal prejudice or bias out of the proceedings. It is clear that many tribunals tried to do just this and it was generally agreed that these tribunals were much fairer than those of 1916–18, but even so there were huge variations in the way they operated and there were many instances of hostility, prejudice and verbal abuse. One example that hit the press headlines, and which was raised in the House of Commons, was that of Judge Richardson, chairman of the Newcastle tribunal, who caused an uproar in October 1939, when he remarked: 'I am certain, as sure as I sit here, that if Christ appeared today he would approve of this war.' According to the report in *The Times*, his comment was met by hisses and boos from the public gallery and proceedings were halted. The judge subsequently apologised and said he had had a long and tiring day.

Matters at the Newcastle tribunal did not improve and in February 1940 Labour MP Frederick Pethick-Lawrence, husband of former suffragette Emmeline Pethick-Lawrence, raised the matter of tribunals in the House of Commons, referring once again to the Newcastle tribunal. He acknowledged that tribunals had an exceedingly difficult task and most were doing their work as well as possible but there were instances where proceedings were 'undignified' and 'unseemly'. He quoted a case at the Newcastle tribunal where when men with the names Donald, Cameron and Douglas were called, Judge Richardson had commented: 'Good fighting names. I think some of the holders of these names would turn in their coffins if they heard what present holders of these names were now saying.' On another occasion, observers recorded the same judge saying to conscientious objectors: 'It is a pity we cannot put you people on a desert island so you could all enjoy yourselves.' This was hardly an example of impartiality, any more than a comment by Sheriff Brown at one of the Scottish tribunals, who said to applicants, 'We will call you the new contemptibles.'

'Even if you get absolute exemption here the State has the power to do with you whatever it thinks fit. They will probably shoot you if you refuse to do anything.' Judge Richardson, Newcastle Conscientious Objector Tribunal, 22 May 1940.

(*The Tribunal*, June 1940)

Treated more rudely

Women also registered as conscientious objectors though in fewer numbers, partly because employment exchanges were reluctant to register female conscientious objectors. Those who did register under the National Service (No 2) Act were usually offered work on the land or in hospitals and only if a woman refused that did she have to appear before a tribunal. On 2 April 1942 Joyce Allen, a PPU member, became the first woman conscientious objector to appear before a tribunal: 'When conscription came in I was teaching. I could have asked for exemption, but I wanted to register as a CO ... They asked me all sorts of questions and I was quite keen to answer them.' Joyce was told to continue teaching but then found herself featured in the press under headlines such as 'Girl conchie teaches boys' and 'Girl conchie attacks British constitution'. The press also hassled her headmaster, wanting to know if he would sack her for being a conscientious objector, but he did not. Joyce Allen received more than 40 supportive letters, some of them from men serving in the RAF: 'I think they were scared out of their wits, these young chaps dropping bombs and wished they could get out of it.'

Just over 1,000 women appeared before their local tribunals and some felt that they were treated more rudely than men. When Connie Bolam, an absolutist, appeared before her tribunal, the chairman, the somewhat infamous Judge Richardson, was extremely hostile, saying, 'We on the tribunal have some common sense and you have none.' Hearing this, members of the public began a slow handclap. The chairman ordered the court to be cleared but no one moved. Eventually the police were brought in. Apparently Judge Richardson was not at all keen on women COs; he told the Hexham Rotary Club that young women objectors were more poisonous than young men and much more assertive. On another occasion about 20 members of the public marched out in protest when Hazel Kerr was told at her tribunal that if she carried her conscientious objection to its logical conclusion she should eat nothing and starve to death. The tribunal chairman then commented 'That might be the most useful thing you could do.'

On trial

Conscientious objectors were not criminals: they had the legal right to apply for exemption. Nevertheless many said that appearing at a tribunal was like being on trial. Eric Farley's tribunal hearing took place in January 1940 and in his view the atmosphere was fairly hostile: 'I appeared ... to state my case before the tribunal in Great Portland Street on an achingly cold and snowy day. The tribunal was, I think, composed of a chairman, who was a judge, and two lay members. The atmosphere was of a criminal court, or so it felt to me, most of the questioning having an antagonistic note and coming from the judge who was also the prosecutor. The defence, so to speak, was conducted by myself ... I do remember being asked why I should persist with views not shared by [Winston] Churchill and other eminent leaders. It was also ferreted out from my written statement, which the tribunal had before them, that I had not joined the PPU until after the war had begun. Much was made of this as if it was a devious ploy. Whatever the reason, I was struck off the register of conscientious objectors and made available for military service.'

By contrast William Charles Elliot, who had been more worried about registering than appearing before a tribunal, found the experience reasonably easy: 'I wasn't unduly worried ... it was a curious thing. It was a very foggy morning and I had to travel from Reigate to Fulham ... I only just got there in time and there was a commissionaire chap on the door whose accent was extremely difficult to follow but I gathered ... that I had to go up the stairs and turn to the right. If I had any private papers to take them out of their envelopes and hand them up to the judge ... I was asked a number of questions. I wasn't asked the traditional question about what would happen if some German soldier raped my wife or something like that, I was spared those questions. I was given exemption, the only condition was that I should continue with the job that I had already started doing, running the hostel for the conscientious objectors who were being placed by Henry Carter's movement, so that all passed off pretty easily really ... they didn't seem hostile to me. I went and sat at the back afterwards and there was hostility shown to some which I thought was very unfair but I didn't sense hostility shown to me ... they weren't affable. I thought they were trying to do an impossible job to the best of their ability. Who can judge another man's conscience? It wasn't a terrible ordeal really; the anticipation was worse than the actual experience of the tribunal.'

Tony Parker was asked some of the 'traditional' questions: 'what would you do if you saw a German soldier trying to rape your sister and all those things and they wouldn't accept the answer, which seems to me to be the only logical answer, "I don't know what I would do." Several others I can't remember. "Do you eat meat?" was one, "so it's alright to kill animals." "If a wasp stung you, would you kill it?" I sometimes thought the whole thing was an illogical exercise. How can you ever judge how somebody's sincere, which is what they were trying to judge. I've no idea.'

His tribunal was in Manchester and he arrived in a fairly emotional state because his father, whom he had visited in hospital the previous day, was gravely ill and had undergone a serious operation: 'I found it very difficult indeed. I was in a very emotional state ... [I] found it very difficult to make any kind of coherent statement as to my objections because anyway they were not really logically thought through, they were a kind of emotional upsurge of feelings, laced with a few quotations from Aldous Huxley, typical 18 or whatever it was-year-old stance ... I remember I was asked "Did I have any religious objections?" and I said I didn't have any religion and they said "You don't believe in life after death?" and I said "No, I don't believe in life after death" and they said "What possible reason can you have for talking about the sanctity of human life?" and I said, "Well that's the reason why I feel human life is sacred because there isn't life after death." Which they thought was extremely illogical … but it was not any intellectual, carefully thought out theory at all and I remember twice bursting into tears while giving my statement and it was perfectly obvious to them that here was somebody who wasn't very reasonable at all, but highly emotional and they gave me exemption on condition that I went into either the Pioneer Corps or the ambulance service.' It was rather unusual for a tribunal to recommend the Pioneer Corps, which was an army unit, but in the event, Tony Parker went on to make an appeal.

After his tribunal, Tony Parker went back to his father's bookshop and a friend, Walter, telephoned to find out how the tribunal had gone. It demonstrates Tony's state of mind that when his friend encouraged him to 'hold on', Tony Parker continued holding onto the telephone for quite some while until he slowly realised what his friend had meant.

Variations

The experience of appearing in front of a tribunal varied considerably depending on the attitude of panel judges, how well an applicant put his or her case, and even on what time of day the tribunal took place. Conscientious objectors and their advisers soon found that some tribunals were more sympathetic than others.

English teacher Ronald Mallone went to Southampton for his tribunal hearing. 'Of that tribunal, the most unpleasant was Dover-Wilson. He always used to ask educational questions. Whoever was before him, he would say, "To what standard were you educated? Did you go to grammar school? Did you pass matric?" … If they mentioned anything about history, he'd say, "How can you tell us anything about history when you didn't even have your matriculation?" I happened to have a first-class degree in history. As soon as he discovered that, he didn't ask me any questions at all. I felt this was very unfair: he was picking on the uneducated … They also varied as to the attitude of the CO and how many raids we'd had the night before. If there had been a raid the night before, the judge was always in a bad temper and antagonistic; if there had been a peaceful night, he was more like a judge.'

COs were helped by having testimonials and witnesses to testify to their sincerity and depth of belief, but surprisingly it was not always necessary to be absolutely articulate. Some tribunals took their commitment to establishing truth and sincerity quite seriously and the results could be unexpected. Some conscientious objectors arrived at their tribunal in a very nervous state and the outcomes were unpredictable. Doris Nicholls was a pacifist, social worker and general secretary of the Fellowship of Reconciliation. She, like several members of the PPU and CBCO, provided support and advice: 'Many of those coming before tribunals were only 18 and some of those poor little devils weren't articulate. But the remarkable thing was that eight times out of ten, the tribunal members not only saw through those who were being smooth … but they also got through to the inarticulate. One I shall never forget, a young man who could … have got exemption on medical grounds but who was a convinced pacifist and felt this was not fair and that he ought to go to the tribunal. When he got there he was literally struck dumb. One question after another came. And there were these great silences … they were kind, they realised the lad could not find enough moisture in his mouth to utter … I was there to speak on his behalf and the chairman turned to me and said, "Can you help us?" … they gave him unconditional exemption.'

As experience mounted conscientious objectors soon learned which tribunals gave fairer hearings than others. To this extent it became something of a postcode lottery. The Fulham tribunal gained a reputation for being very unsympathetic to conscientious objectors applying for unconditional or absolute exemption and its chairman was well known for bullying tactics. By contrast, the South Eastern tribunal was considered to be much fairer.

Provocative questioning
By and large tribunals looked most sympathetically on conscientious objectors who put forward religious beliefs. Quakers for instance were almost invariably given exemption from military service, so much so that some Quakers preferred – initially at least – not to define themselves by their faith. Brian Phillips was born in 1924 and was a Quaker and a pacifist. His father had been a churchwarden in the Anglican Church and registered as a conscientious objector during the First World War. After the war, disgusted by what he felt was the militarism of the Anglicans, he became a Quaker, and all his children, including Brian, were brought up as Quakers. Brian was about 15 when war broke out and studying science at grammar school. Aged 17

he could have gone on to university but decided that 'to go to university in the wartime conditions and the general malevolence within our society as a result of the war' would not be appropriate. He started work on the land, at an organic farm, and in 1942, when his age group was due to be called up, registered as a conscientious objector. In due course he appeared before a tribunal: 'By that stage tribunals had got used to Quakers and it was really pretty simple, once I revealed the fact that I was a Quaker. I didn't at first because I thought in a sense that would be cheating. I just put forward the pacifist position without mentioning religion and said I was convinced that war was no way to settle disputes.' His views were not very well received by the tribunal: 'they said "What is your religious conviction?" because I hadn't mentioned it and at that point I had to confess that I was a Quaker and from then on it was plain sailing – conditional exemption, conditional on continuing to work on the land.'

Mervyn Taggart was also a Quaker: 'My position was very much easier than most because people understood the Quaker position, it was a historical one, and this made it relatively easy at the tribunal ... I was one of a very, very small number who were given unconditional exemption. That means they left it to me to do what I thought was right during the war.'

However, even those conscientious objectors who had deeply held religious beliefs found themselves being quizzed on certain aspects of their beliefs. They were asked which church they belonged to, how long they had attended and, if they produced Biblical references to back up their arguments, had these challenged. Some judges pointed out that the leaders of the Church of England and Catholic churches backed the war and quoted Biblical references back at applicants in an attempt to undermine their views. Applicants such as Len Richardson commented that panel members often demanded the names of the 12 apostles, and many COs found that if they quoted Biblical references to back up their beliefs, panel members would produce counter references.

Reginald Bottini appeared before the Fulham tribunal: 'I will never forget my tribunal because I was trembling, trembling more with indignation than anything else. It was Fulham, which was credited as being very, very harsh on COs. Seven lads who were obviously religious fanatics of various kinds went before me one by one; they all based their objections on the Bible. It struck me that the members of the tribunal seemed to have a list of counter-quotations from the holy book so that when one of these unfortunates quoted the saying, "That if thine enemy strike thee on the right cheek turn unto him the left," they only had to turn up counter-statement number 26, "And he took whips and beat the money-lenders out of the temple". They were all refused registration as COs and ordered to be transcribed on the military register. So I became convinced that when my number was called that I would be dealt with in a similar fashion. And in a rather confused and inarticulate way, I adopted the most aggressive posture to their questioning. In fact they gave me conditional registration, the only one out of eight. I reached the conclusion, cynical youngster that I was, that it wasn't on the basis of conscience at all, but that here they saw a red-haired trouble-maker of Irish/Italian descent that might be difficult for army discipline.'

Some faith groups were discriminated against, chief among them being the Jehovah's Witnesses, whose beliefs confused and at times irritated tribunals as well as other COs. Most tribunal members had difficulty in coming to terms with the beliefs of Jehovah's Witnesses, whose first duty was to the kingdom of God and who took a 'neutral' stance when it came to human affairs. Douglas Beavor was a Jehovah's Witness, who took an absolutist stand: 'I am not a pacifist, the war of Armageddon I would support, although not by bearing arms or taking part, but I would be in complete agreement with it … At the beginning Jehovah's Witnesses were recognised as conscientious objectors and were given exemption, but that changed after about a year and after that we were not recognised as conscientious objectors. The pressure was on after Dunkirk and our stand, being absolute, brought down the wrath of the authorities on us.'

When it came to political or humanitarian objectors, tribunals used particularly challenging and provocative questions, frequently appearing to probe applicants' social consciences by asking things like 'Don't you realise that many of your old school friends are risking their lives to defend you?' or 'Would you not defend your wife/mother/friend if they were attacked?'. By and large tribunals were least sympathetic to political objectors, particularly if they considered that the applicant was not necessarily opposed to war in general, but to the current war specifically. Many political objectors, who were usually socialists or communists, who might take up arms in support of a working-class revolution – Spain was the obvious example – had their applications rejected out of hand, which in 1940 caused the two Labour MPs Alfred Salter and Arthur Creech Jones to complain to the Secretary of State. The situation was confused and in November 1939 in the House of Commons Reginald Sorensen MP had asked the Minister of Labour whether tribunals were discriminating between objectors who based their views on religious, ethical or political grounds. The reply was vague but following further questions, it appeared that political objection did come within the scope of the conscience clause.

As early as December 1939 there had been a test case when an objector George Plume, a member of the Independent Labour Party (ILP) who had been given conditional exemption by his local tribunal, appeared at an appeal tribunal because the Ministry itself had overturned the local tribunal's decision. Fenner Brockway represented Plume at the appellate tribunal. The Ministry's view was that Plume, as a political objector, could not be said to be a genuine conscientious objector: 'this applicant would be perfectly prepared to engage in a class war and, if necessary, to shed blood.' Putting George Plume's case, Fenner Brockway argued that it was an extraordinarily difficult thing to judge a man's conscience but in his opinion it came down to where a man's 'inner loyalty lies'. He argued that 'just as there may be that loyalty to God which may make a man a complete pacifist, just as there may be loyalty to a nation, George has a loyalty to the working-class of every country … Nowhere in the Act does it say that it is only the man who has pacifist convictions, or religious convictions, or ethical convictions; nowhere in the whole Act does it rule out the man whose conscientiousness may be equally sincere but who is entirely a political objector.' In the event the Ministry's appeal was upheld and Plume's name was removed from the register of conscientious objectors and put on the military register.

Interestingly, Plume was told by H.A.L. Fisher at his appeal tribunal that the decision would have gone easier with him if he had described himself as a pacifist, something that Plume wrote to *Peace News* about: 'I should like to make my issue clear. I loathe all forms of war, including the class war. I therefore (to carry my argument to its logical conclusion) strive for a classless system of Socialism which would eliminate all war and its causes. This in my opinion is the correct Pacifist Perspective. But this war is a Capitalist War waged in the interests of Capitalism, therefore I must oppose it as such. At the

Tribunal I was told by the Rt. Hon. H.A.L. Fisher that it would be so much easier for me if I pleaded as a Pacifist. But the right of a political objector to conscientiously object to this war had to be fought ... The case was lost—but lost fighting. COs must unite against this inhuman denial of man's right to his own conscience.' Despite this case, local tribunals continued to make their own decisions and while most dismissed political objectors, others granted exemptions, either conditionally or unconditionally.

However, given the baffling and sometimes antagonistic questioning, it is not surprising that some applicants lost patience with tribunals. According to Fred Vahey's daughter Lorna, her father became so exasperated with the questions hurled at him that he just threw his papers down and stormed out of the tribunal. To this day the family is still uncertain exactly what happened. According to Lorna: 'We were told these stories so often you were never quite sure whether that is what happened, or whether you assumed it was what happened ... He said you had to go in, read out your statement, or it was read out, they would then question you and you were only allowed to answer "yes" or "no" and my father in his life had never answered only yes or no. He then tried to explain but they shut him up, so he threw the paper at them and walked out. And that was that.' Apparently Fred heard no more from the authorities; according to Lorna 'either he got lost in the paperwork somehow or they thought he was more trouble than he was worth ... Maybe it was because he had a little patch of land ... but I think that it was the general muddle because he just walked out and I've always admired that.' Whatever the reason, Fred was then left alone, although he did experience some hostility locally. COs often felt they were in a parallel universe where tribunal members just did not understand them at all. And there were many who, in the words of one CO, 'failed to get the tribunal to understand what my real point of view was'.

Categories

As well as assessing the sincerity of an individual's conscience, tribunal panels also needed to establish into which category a CO should be placed. By law tribunals had four options: they could grant unconditional exemption from military service (category A); exemption from military service conditional on doing alternative civilian service, which might include work on the land, civil defence, or hospital work (category B); to register a conscientious objector on the military register but for non-combatant duties only (category C); or to dismiss an applicant completely and place him on the military register (category D).

The most controversial option and the one least likely to be granted was unconditional exemption. Denis Hayes took an unconditional stand – also sometimes known as an absolutist position. He took a prepared statement to his tribunal: 'It was more or less quotations. I didn't say anything particularly personal. I was taking the unconditional stand … the chairman apparently said under his voice that I was "a broken reed" and they came back and announced that they had registered me unconditionally.'

Denis Hayes was unusual; of the approximately 62,000 conscientious objectors who appeared before local tribunals, only about 2,900 were granted absolute unconditional exemption and there were considerable regional differences. As already mentioned, the Fulham tribunal was the least sympathetic, so much so that its judge, Judge Drucquer, commented on two occasions that he was not empowered to grant unconditional exemption, which was completely incorrect and was challenged by the CBCO. Overall the numbers of unconditional exemptions dropped sharply as the war progressed. In 1939, 14 per cent of all applicants got unconditional exemption from local tribunals; by 1940 as the war intensified and German troops occupied much of Europe, the percentage dropped to five per cent and by 1941 only two per cent of applicants were granted absolute exemption. Similarly the overall number of conscientious objectors applying to local tribunals also dropped as the war progressed.

Most applicants – around 23,600 or nearly 38 per cent of the total – were given conditional exemption. Another 17,200 were given

Decisions of local tribunals	Men	Women	Total	% of total
Unconditional exemption	2,868	69	2,937	4.7
Conditional exemption	22,949	689	23,638	37.9
Non-combatant in forces	17,193	38	17,231	27.7
Removed from CO register	18,217	278	18,495	29.7

Source: *Challenge of Conscience*, Denis Hayes (Allen & Unwin, 1949)

category C and about 18,400 applicants, nearly 30 per cent, had their cases dismissed and were removed from the register of conscientious objectors, making them liable for call-up into the forces as combatants.

Appeal tribunals

Applicants who were not satisfied with the decision of the tribunals could go to appeal. There were two appellate courts, one for England and Wales, which was in London, and one for Scotland. Panels for appellate courts consisted of a chairman and two other members, described by Denis Hayes as the 'three wise men'. The chairman of the London appellate court was the respected Oxford historian H.A.L. Fisher. About 10,800 conscientious objectors disagreed with local tribunal decisions and took their cases to appeal. Nearly 6,000 failed to get their decisions overturned. They were removed from the register of conscientious objectors and many of the men found themselves liable for combatant duties in the forces. Some accepted their fate; others resisted.

Chapter 5

On the Land

'This was my first experience of physical activity so unremitting, so ruthlessly mechanical.'

Edward Blishen

Nearly 2,900 conscientious objectors received unconditional exemption. Once tribunals had reached this decision, neither they nor the government had any further responsibility for them. How they spent the war years varied. Denis Hayes worked with the CBCO; Fred Vahey remained on his smallholding in Pett, East Sussex, living in a Romany caravan with his wife Zoe, creating the self-sufficient lifestyle that was his aim. There were attempts to persuade him into civil defence duties, which he refused to do, but otherwise he was left alone. Kenneth and Mary Wray similarly attempted to farm their land, worked on orchards and refused to register for national identity or ration cards. Wray later did get a ration card and said he had let his principles down badly by doing so. Some joined farming communities, others continued in the work or activities they had been doing before the war, although many discovered their employers did not want to keep them on staff, and so they were forced to find other occupations. Quite a few also took up humanitarian work.

Conditional exemption
By far the greatest number of conscientious objectors – 23,638 according to Denis Hayes – was given exemption conditional on doing work of national importance, under civilian control. It was a sensible decision: from 1940, following the end of the 'phoney war', Britain organised for 'total war', which meant mobilising civilians just as

much as soldiers. Propaganda urged civilians on the home front to 'do their bit' for the war effort, whether this meant working on the land, in munitions factories, growing vegetables, clearing bombed out houses, providing aid in shelters, fighting fires or driving ambulances. The problem with conscientious objectors, however, was to find employment that on the one hand did not contravene their principles, but on the other hand contributed to the national need. It was not an easy situation, not least because conscientious objectors often met opposition and prejudice from would-be employers and as war intensified and conditions worsened for Britain, public resentment of conscientious objectors increased. At the same time COs themselves had differing views about what activities they saw as colluding with the war and which did not. Stella St John, for instance, worked with down and outs during the war but also volunteered to do ambulance driving during the height of the Blitz. 'I did it in a voluntary capacity … perhaps it would [be classified as war work] … it was a civilian organisation. It's impossible to opt completely out of it [the war] … you find that out paying taxes … you eat food that's brought in on a convoy … you can't opt out … just do the best you can.'

The type of work that conscientious objectors should do and how much they should be paid was the subject of debate among tribunals, the Ministry of Labour, the CBCO and trade unions. Opinions differed. Sometimes tribunals recommended that conscientious objectors should continue in the work they were doing, particularly if it was teaching, scientific research, farming or social work. More usually though tribunals recommended alternative employment, specifically work considered to be of national importance, such as farming, forestry, hospital work and civil defence. This often meant that the CO had to move some distance from home, but the general view was that as everyone's lives were being dramatically changed by the impact of war, COs should be making the same sacrifices as men in the forces. The issue of pay and conditions was problematic. The general feeling was that no conscientious objector should earn more than a man in the forces and there was discussion of introducing legislation for this purpose. In the end the Trades Union Congress (TUC) refused to have anything to do with the proposal, which undermined the basic trade union principle of paying a man or woman the 'rate for the job'.

As a result in February 1941 Ernest Bevin, Minister of Labour and National Service, announced that the government would not proceed with implementing legislation to carry the proposal through. Even so, the aim of tribunals was not just to place conscientious objectors in essential work, but also to ensure the conditions they experienced should not be better than those experienced by men in the forces. In some instances tribunals paid attention to the type of work COs offered to do, provided it was not seen as too comfortable or convenient, but by and large they were influenced by government directives and what was needed at the time. Once tribunals had directed conscientious objectors into certain areas of work, it was up to COs to find the jobs themselves. Those who failed to do so risked being recalled by the tribunal, penalised and having their conscientious objector status overturned.

Land work

Thousands of conscientious objectors were directed into work on the land. They did work such as land reclamation, ditching, drainage and general heavy farming work. Farming had been seriously depressed during the inter-war years, and by 1939 there was an urgent need for neglected farmland to be brought back into production. Before the war Britain had imported around 70 per cent of its foodstuffs, and with war underway and the waters bristling with German U-boats, it was essential to increase food production at home. Initially farming was on the list of reserved occupations but as war progressed this changed and with more and more farm workers leaving to go and fight, there was a growing need for workers. Members of the Women's Land Army, the unemployed and conscientious objectors were seen as potential sources of agricultural workers. In December 1940 an editorial in *The Times* under the heading 'This Fertile Island' suggested that 'Labour gangs should be recruited from any farm workers who are unemployed, from conscientious objectors and refugee aliens who can be sent under experienced foremen to carry out the necessary clearing of ditches and drains so that the land may again produce to the full.'

Finding work meant either going onto privately run farms or applying for jobs with one of the War Agricultural Committees established in each county. Despite the crying need for workers, conscientious objectors often had difficulty in finding a job, largely because most farmers did not want to use them. The National Farmers Union (NFU), who equally resisted women workers at the start of the war, resented farms being used as a type of dumping ground for 'conchies'. Farmers not only felt that they would be incapable of doing the hard labour but also did not want to use men who were frequently viewed as unpatriotic shirkers. The Dorset branch of the NFU summed up the situation in December 1939 when it passed a resolution stating that conscientious objectors should not be allowed to work on the land because 'they did not make good workers and the farmers resented agriculture being regarded as an easy stop gap to avoid military service'. Other NFU branches passed similar resolutions, so time and again conscientious objectors applied for jobs only to be turned down. As late as June 1941 a conscientious objector wrote to *Farmers Weekly* complaining that he had applied for 40 jobs without success. The Ministry of Labour urged farmers to put their prejudices to one side and, as the need for extra workers increased, farmers found themselves having to employ COs.

By April 1942 there were 7,295 conditionally exempted conscientious objectors employed in agriculture. Some found work through personal contacts. Brian Phillips already had farming experience, working in Norfolk on what was possibly the first commercial organic farm in England. He had also worked on the home farm of a Rudolph Steiner community. After registering as a conscientious objector in 1942, and gaining exemption provided he continued working on the land, Brian's brother offered him a job: 'My brother Merlin had by that time got a farm, a dairy farm near Exeter and he was having problems getting anyone to work on the farm. The War Ag Committee wouldn't let him have a land girl because he was a conscientious objector ... it was about seven or eight miles out of Exeter up in the hills, so he appealed to me to go and help him out because he was having to work seven days a week non-stop. It wasn't a big farm but there was no let up ... so I worked with him for a time until again the War Ag Committee intervened and said "Sorry you can't stay here, you can have a land girl but you can't stay here" ... so I had to move out.' Having been expelled from his brother's farm, Brian went to join two progressive schools working on their kitchen gardens until a well-known Quaker and psychiatric social worker David Wills invited him to work at Bodenham Manor, Herefordshire, which was being developed as a home for delinquent boys and girls.

Similarly, Christadelphian Len Richardson found work on the land through personal contacts: 'It happened that an elderly Christadelphian owned a fruit and vegetable business in the town, and bought supplies from a local grower about three miles away. Through his good offices, I eventually got work in these market gardens, which were fairly extensive.' He was very apprehensive when he set off on his bicycle to start work, expecting hostility from the other farm workers.

The majority of COs were placed on the land by the War Agricultural Committees, who supplied farms with workers, often organising them into mobile work gangs that travelled around the countryside doing hard, manual work such as ditching, threshing and digging drains. Writer Edward Blishen started his work on the land with the Essex War Agricultural Committee and was moved several times during the war, threshing, digging ditches and working as a driver's mate.

Hard manual labour

Most conscientious objectors had never done any farming before the war and had little idea of the harsh manual work involved. Nor was any training provided; instead they had to learn on the job, often under the direction of a foreman who was not necessarily sympathetic to them. Wages too were much lower than most objectors, many of whom had been in white-collar jobs, had been receiving before the war. This worsened after 1940, when the Agricultural Wages Board lowered the minimum rates payable to inexperienced workers from 48 shillings a week to 38 shillings.

COs who did not know better viewed farming in a rather romantic manner, assuming that no special skills would be necessary but the reality turned out to be quite different. For those who exchanged desk and pen for billhooks and tractors, work on the land came as something of a shock. Len Richardson had been an insurance clerk before the war and had not expected just how challenging labouring on the land would be: 'There seems to be a feeling that industry, or the white-collar jobs, calls for special skills, whereas anybody can do jobs on the land. I was to learn, however, that this is far from the truth, and the simple skills of hoeing, planting, picking, hedging, ditching take a long time and much practice, before the raw recruit from an urban background can begin to compete with his rural counterpart.' Len was not the only one to feel this way. Ernest Goldring had worked in a bank: 'after working in a bank, farm work was pretty tough. I never had been particularly robust in health, so at the physical level it was certainly very exhausting and demanding. In addition to which, we had to look after ourselves: cook, wash our clothes, empty the loo bucket.' As time went on though, Goldring came to enjoy the rural surroundings and learned new skills such as milking, ploughing and digging.

One CO who wrote about his wartime experiences on the land was Edward Blishen. Although his father had served in the First World War and was opposed to his pacifist views, Blishen registered as a conscientious objector in 1940. He went before his tribunal in London and was given exemption, conditional on doing land work. At that point, he was working as a reporter with the *Monmouth Hill Standard*. In 1941, together with five other conscientious objectors, Blishen was sent by the War Ag Committee to the small village of Cold Clapton in Essex, near the North Sea, to begin 'ditching, hedging and land clearance'. Describing himself as 'quite a weedy intellectual type', Blishen had to grapple with billhooks and scythes, digging ditches and slashing away at hedges. During the first few days, when he was attempting to cut down blackberry bushes, he was described as 'cack-handed' by the foreman, a phrase Blishen used for the title of his book *A Cack-handed War*. For Blishen, as for most conscientious objectors, doing hard manual work out in all weathers was a huge physical strain: 'It was all thorns and icy water. We cleared the fields, and reduced the hedges to the simplicity of wounded stumps. We dug new ditches, and began to find some moments good: when, for instance, sections of a ditch were joined, and the damned-up water began to sing down it. It was … like an enormous piece of spring-cleaning … but it was, in fact, *winter*-cleaning. In the mornings I woke with fingers crooked in the shape they'd taken round the bagging-hook or spade the day before. The icy water entered my bones … my whole skeleton would ache. I could feel the ice in every bone.'

No matter how tough the work, conscientious objectors rarely felt they were in any position to complain about the conditions. John Petts was sent to Derbyshire where one of his tasks was to move quicklime: 'The farm manager said, "Today we're carting quicklime and don't forget it's bloody quick!" He meant corrosive, the sort of lime they dissolved bodies in during the Great Plague. My body started to dissolve too. There was always this wind and rain. You marked the field out and placed these pyramids of pure white … across the field. The wind was blowing this corrosive dust about and the rain was wetting my face. I had two livid lines from my eyes straight down my face ... I felt I would be scarred for the rest of my life ... nothing was said about my burns. It was impossible to complain. The answer would be, "You shut your mouth; men are dying out there".'

Prejudice and criticism

There was a world of difference between most conscientious objectors and the farmers and labourers that they worked among. As Edward Blishen described, even their appearance singled them out: 'A batch of us had come the previous day, and we saw them at work in a field near the road, and climbed through a hedge to meet them. There was no difficulty at all in deciding that they were not normal land workers. One or two wore trilbies that had plainly been in tube trains, and other urban situations. One was wearing a college scarf; another plus-fours. They were all talking – another mark of the town – and there was in that first moment when we saw them, something in the hesitations of the sickles and billhooks they were using, in the way they seemed to be hacking away without clear purpose.'

Some conscientious objectors were apprehensive about how they would be treated. Len Richardson, setting out on his bicycle on his first morning on the farm, was anxious: 'As I cycled out of town the first morning, I had very serious misgivings. I had heard tales of what happened to COs working on the land, some had been beaten up (a friend of mine had been) and others had been thrown into the village pond ... I felt myself to be riding, rather ingloriously, into the jaws of certain persecution.'

As it happened, Len Richardson did not experience the hostility that he expected, but many did. When Edward Blishen arrived in his lodgings, it was clear that the landlady, although outwardly friendly, was not happy having conscientious objectors billeted on her and one of Blishen's companions noticed four white feathers in a vase on the mantelpiece – the white feather being a mark of cowardice common in the First World War. Blishen remained working on the land on different jobs and farms until discharged in 1946 and encountered hostility from time to time, though it was verbal rather than physical. One farmer referred to him and his colleagues as 'Bloody rats, traitors and yellow-bellies' and did not want to employ them, until the War Ag Committee representative persuaded him saying they were good workers. Within minutes of arriving on another farm, the bailiff displayed his dislike of 'conchies' by announcing that they should not be allowed to marry and listed various islands to which they should be sent before saying that he would like to push them into a trusser or mechanical hay baler.

One conscientious objector who encountered brutality was Ronald Smith. A Christian who profoundly believed that war 'was just not right. How could a Christian go out killing people?', Ronald was 24 when he registered as a conscientious objector. After Ronald's case was reported in the local paper in Glastonbury, one local shop refused to serve him. Given conditional exemption and directed to find land work, he left his office job and started looking for work: 'I had done six years work on my father's farm so I thought I could cope, but this farmer was terrible. In a field one day, he was about to lash me with a horsewhip, but I stood my ground and told him he dare not do it, and he slowly calmed down.' Smith became ill but the doctor refused to treat him because he was a conscientious objector. Subsequently Ronald Smith joined a Christian pacifist forestry and land unit.

There were several complaints that conscientious objectors made poor agricultural workers. In May 1941 a Major Carlos Clarke of Sussex wrote to *The Times* complaining about 12 conscientious objectors whom he had employed via the Surrey War Agricultural Committee for drainage work. According to him, they were 'strong young men between the ages of 20 and 30,' who' had no idea how to work, and appeared to have no desire to learn'. According to his account, the foreman, who had been chosen by the conscientious objectors, had 'no qualifications for the work whatever' and a job that should have taken only two weeks had already taken two months and had not yet been completed. This view of laziness and inefficiency was echoed in some sections of the press: on 21 May 1944 headlines in the *Sunday Express* stormed 'Farmers rage at "Sunbathing Conchies". They spend their time behind the hedges reading. They cannot be sacked for loafing.'

This reaction was not surprising. Some COs resented the hard manual work, the monotony, boredom, and servitude of life on the land, particularly those who were being directed by the War Ag Committees, and made no secret of the fact, although those who actively avoided working were very few in number. Most problems stemmed from the objectors' lack of skills and complete unfamiliarity with farming and rural traditions. According to Lorna Vahey, her father Fred, working on his own smallholding, was astounded by just how 'cack-handed' conscientious objectors were when it came to digging and hoeing – he also commented on the fact that most of them preferred to stand around and talk. The problem was that of two different worlds: as Edward Blishen commented, the farm worker tended to work hard in silence, 'the conchie, with his horrible habit of asking questions and his general passion for talk,' did not fit easily into that environment and was often resented.

Even so, most did the best they could and as time passed attitudes began to change, particularly during the Blitz, when it became clear that civilians were just as much risk of death and injury as soldiers at the front. Conscientious objectors were also proving their worth. On 20 May 1941 a letter appeared in *The Times* from C. Porteous, Labour Officer, with the County Institute of Agriculture, Preston, saying that he wanted to put on record that the conscientious objectors employed by the Lancashire War Agricultural Executive Committee 'have worked well and willingly'. In 1941 the *Preston Guardian* also commented that objectors were carrying out 'marvellous' drainage work and said the paper had to respect the principles of men who were prepared to go to extremes, such as wading waist deep into icy water, to prove them.

On a personal level, the experience of land work varied. Stuart Smith registered as a conscientious objector in 1940. He believed 'that wars could be ended, and could only be ended by men refusing to fight in them; because of this the right thing to do was to refuse to fight ... I felt it was wrong of a society to impose sacrifice ... on its own members for its own protection ... I saw war as wrong and conscription as another wrong.' Stuart appeared before his tribunal in October but his application was rejected and his appeal upheld the decision. He was placed on the military register and subsequently imprisoned for not attending his medical examination. When he came out of prison in 1942 he joined a group of COs working under the local War Agricultural Committee.

For Stuart the work was 'peaceful, tiring, boring and rather futile' and his aim was just to get through it. But some objectors gained a deep insight into a way of life they had not known before. Edward Blishen 'noticed an effect of this endless manual labour: that now, when I saw a knot tied somewhere, anything heaped up, I thought of the men whose toil lay behind the knot or heap. I became aware of the enormous boring daily labours on which the whole world rested. I thought solemnly that after years of middle-class schooling and then three years of petty journalism, this was a knowledge I needed to have. I hoped it was one I should not forget, if ever, for me, there came an end to it.'

Christian Pacifist Forestry and Land Units

A number of pacifist groups were created during the war to help conscientious objectors find work. In 1939 Rev. Henry Carter, a Methodist and pacifist, who had founded the Methodist Peace Fellowship, set up the Christian Pacifist Forestry and Land Units (CPFLU). He had the approval of Ernest Brown, Minister of Labour and National Service, himself a devout Nonconformist. Rev. Carter aimed to provide work for three categories of religious conscientious objectors: those who had been directed into land work but could not find it because farmers would not employ them; those whose firms had switched to war work that they could not in conscience undertake; and those who had been sacked from their jobs because they were pacifists. Carter contacted the Forestry Commission and it was agreed that the Commission would employ conscientious objectors; the first unit was set up in Hemstead Forest, Kent, where workers lived in a large, derelict house. Work opportunities with the Forestry Commission increased and by 1940 there were units in Sussex, Hampshire and the Forest of Dean.

William Elliot had been working as an insurance agent before the war and had been actively involved with the No More War Movement (NMWM) in Guildford during the late 1920s, organising processions and speakers, then subsequently became branch secretary of the PPU. He moved to Reigate, where in 1937, he became a Labour councillor. He also made links with Henry Carter's Methodist Pacifist Group. Following the creation of the CPFLU a young pastor asked him to find a hostel for conscientious objectors in Reigate. He rang up the borough surveyor who provided a list of unoccupied properties. Henry Carter came down and they found 'a pretty awful old house ... but it served the purpose ... we got 20 men into this house, not much room, had to keep the basement as an air raid shelter.'

Carter needed a married warden to run the hostel and Elliot and his wife took the job. They had to furnish the hostel as simply and cheaply as possible, allowing for five or six men to a room. When the hostel was finished, the men were 'not enjoying any better conditions than they would have done if they had been in the army, and probably not as good'. Elliot's tribunal hearing came up while he was working at the hostel; he received an exemption conditional on continuing his work with the CPFLU.

The conscientious objectors who worked with the CPFLU came from all backgrounds and walks of life. Interviewed by the Imperial War Museum, Elliot said: 'Some of them were a bit fundamentalist, which I found difficult to get on with. It was Christian Pacifist Forestry and Land Units so they had all arrived at their position from the Christian point of view, which didn't mean that living together was any easier than it would have been with any other group of people, and perhaps in a way more difficult because there we were trying to create a community of individuals and people who were very individualistic and perhaps didn't fit in all that easily to a communal atmosphere, but we managed.'

Although Elliot himself was both a Christian and a socialist, he found the more fundamentalist religions a little hard to cope with: 'We had two brothers living in the hostel, splendid chaps, Quakers they were. They spent a Sunday chopping wood which they had managed to get quite legitimately from their work and bring back for use as fuel and some of the Sabbatarian chaps were praying for them, and I felt this would be more logical if they had removed themselves from the fire on which the logs were burning.'

As wardens, Elliot and his wife ran the hostel, liaised with the CPFLU and the employers, and bought and prepared food for the men. As the war progressed, Elliot moved on from running just one hostel to managing 40 or 50 hostels for land workers, not all of whom were conscientious objectors, so he was also managing land girls, Irish labourers, displaced persons (DPs) and volunteer workers as part of a land scheme run by the Ministry of Agriculture. Eventually the CPFLU came under the direct control of the Ministry of Agriculture. During his time on the land, Elliot considered that he met little or no hostility. When an official from the Surrey War Agriculture Committee offered him the job of running a War Agriculture Committee hostel in Guildford: 'I said, "Yes, it complies with my tribunal conditions so, if you don't mind having a conscientious objector, I'm quite willing to do it." And he said something like he didn't give a damn if I was a conscientious objector so long as I could do the job for him.'

Some COs were uncomfortable working on the land because they felt they were colluding with the war effort, but Elliot did not agree. He considered that he expressed his opposition to the war by refusing to take part in it, 'but that didn't mean that I wanted to separate myself from the rest of mankind, quite the opposite'. He was also quite prepared to mix with soldiers, whom he considered were far more sympathetic to conscientious objectors than civilians.

In fact the main instance of hostility he encountered had been in Reigate when he was a local councillor and a council officer refused to give him a lift because of his pacifist views: 'I never found this from soldiers ... I found nothing but friendship among soldiers. I had a great deal to do with them. If there was any army camp nearby we'd try to establish relations with them and invite them over to the hostel for social evenings and they'd invite us back to the camp ... There was one occasion when a whole convoy of soldiers stopped outside the hostel, it was the middle of winter ... so I made cocoa for them and took it up and down the lines and told the chaps at night that I'd used their rations for this and hoped they didn't mind. Most of them were fine but there were one or two who felt their opposition to the war meant they had to be opposed to those who were pursuing it ... I never saw things that way.' On one occasion Elliot, as part of his job, was looking for billets for some CO land workers and encountered a rather unexpected and amusing response: 'I remember going to one lady and she said "So long as it wasn't a conscientious man" – she didn't realise what she was saying, did she?'

After his experience with the violent farmer, Ronald Smith applied to join the CPFLU and was found forestry work in Bruton Forest: 'There were four of us in the Unit – a Roman Catholic, Methodist, Congregationalist and me, Church of England ... The work in the forest was very hard, working with some eight or ten local workers. Thick undergrowth had to be cut down with and burned to clear the ground for planting ... Then we had to plant 400 Norway Spruce trees ... No easy task. We often talked to the next person to us and arguments arose sometimes. One day Reg [local worker] smacked my face really hard. I stood still and told him if it made him feel better to smack the other cheek as well. Slowly he dropped his hands and even said he was sorry ... These men were tough Home Guards and one threatened to bring his gun ... and shoot me. He thought I was a German and my name was Rudolph Schmidt.'

Holton-cum-Beckering

Pacifism and the desire to create a co-operative society based on the land frequently go hand in hand. During the war pacifists either set up communities or went to work on them. One community that combined idealism and practicality was based in the small Lincolnshire village of Holton-cum-Beckering. The PPU, in conjunction with Richard Cornwallis, an accountant, and architect Roy Broadbent, father of Oscar-winning British actor Jim Broadbent, developed the Lincolnshire Farm Training Scheme (LFTS) with the dual aim of training conscientious objectors in land work and at the same time providing pacifists an escape from the over materialistic world. An appeal for donations was launched through *Peace News*, and the money raised bought land and buildings. It was, as Denis Hayes described, 'a feet on the ground attempt to develop a co-operative farming enterprise for conscientious objectors and their families'.

A number of conscientious objectors came to work and live at the community; they included former teachers, tailors, accountants, journalists and artists. Among those who worked and lived at Holton-cum Beckering in its early days was Francis Cammaerts, a teacher and pacifist who registered as a conscientious objector when war began. He was working at the community when he appeared before his tribunal and was exempted, provided he continued on the land. Subsequently through the death of his brother who was serving in the RAF and the birth of his daughter, convinced Francis that he could no longer remain a CO and in 1942 he was recruited into the Special Operations Executive (SOE), the highly secret sabotage organisation, spending the remainder of the war as a British agent in occupied France, organising resistance fighters.

Eric Farley, whose application for conscientious objector status was rejected and who had spent time in Lewes prison for refusing military orders, also came to the community, largely because his brother Victor, who was also a CO and had been sacked from his job, had been involved in setting up the community. Eric's daughter Susannah remembers that 'my Dad went off to my uncle's farm, a community that had been set up in Lincolnshire. There was a whole bunch of people there, all ideological pacifists really, and they all got together on this farm and they were just digging the land and keeping animals.'

Bookbinder Arthur Adams also worked at Holton. For him 'it was nice to find you weren't alone'. Living accommodation was very basic and the work was hard, but for those who lived at Holton the experience was rewarding. Arthur Adams believed that 'on the whole we led useful lives', both producing food and living co-operatively. Local people were somewhat suspicious, believing that the pacifists were communists or spies, and probably both. Gradually suspicions were overcome, not least because the community, which had a rich cultural life, put on plays for the locals. Out of this came the Holton Players, later the Lindsey Rural Players. There was a military airbase nearby and Susannah Farley remembers her father telling her about 'listening to the sounds of the planes going out of the aerodrome and counting the number of engines they could hear going out and the number that would come back. They were all very involved in it. They used to go to the local pub and all the airmen were in the pub and they would mix with the conscientious objectors and there was no animosity.'

Quite a number of pacifist land communities existed before and during the war, among them the Adelphi Centre in Essex, which was co-founded by Max Plowman and John Middleton Murry in 1934. It did not survive but was later taken over by the PPU to accommodate Spanish refugee children. Pacifist communes and communities represented a beautiful dream and a sincere wish to find a peaceful way of life but many were short-lived, some perhaps being too idealistic to survive. For absolutist Mervyn Taggart, who worked at various pacifist land communities: 'I saw these communities as a brave new world, a microcosm of what the world might become: co-operative and thoroughly unselfish, very giving, giving being the very basis of life and progress. I got tremendously caught up with them and ... just worked to the point of exhaustion ... They failed for three reasons ... members didn't always have the necessary technical skills ... there tended to be a conflict of personalities ... [and] ... they didn't provide a totally different economic system.' He believed though, that they had '*tremendous* potential'.

Chapter 6

Mining and Humanitarian Work

'There were many individuals who felt they could not take part in the war as combatants ... who at the same time wished to serve humanity.'
Dr Kenneth Mellanby

Most conditionally exempted conscientious objectors were directed into work on the land, but tribunals also directed them into other civilian work. As the war went on and needs increased, tribunals often suggested a range of alternatives that might include farming, forestry, hospital work, mining and civil defence. The latter was fairly contentious, with many conscientious objectors feeling that it involved too great a collusion with the war machine.

In the mines
As the industrial demands of war gathered pace, there was a growing need for men to work in the mines, and from 1943 the 'Bevin Boys' were formed from men who were actively conscripted into that work. However, even earlier than this some tribunals were directing conscientious objectors into mining, although the CBCO, who felt that coal mining was too closely related to the war effort, lobbied the Minister of Labour to instruct tribunals not to give coal mining as a sole condition of exemption.

According to Tony Parker, his tribunal had recommended that he be sent into the Pioneer Corps, a non-combatant unit with the army. Despite some pressure from his father and sister to give up his CO stance, he was not prepared to comply: 'You were allowed to appeal against the decision and I did, and in due course went to another tribunal, the appellate tribunal, and said I didn't agree with going into

the army. I remember somebody older than me, working with COs …
said to me "try not to be truculent" … I think I quite successfully gave
an impression of someone quiet and reasonable. They gave me
exemption … if I would accept civil defence work, which I was already
doing, or agriculture, or the fire service, or coal mining'.

Tony chose coal mining mainly because he had no knowledge of the
work and decided it would be 'an unusual experience'. He was told to
report to a coal mine in Bradford, which was quite some distance from
his home and because he needed to start work at five am, took lodgings
with a widow, whose husband had been a miner and who did not
mind that he was a conscientious objector. For a young man who
worked in a bookshop, living and working in a mining community
'was a whole new world. I never knew what work was like … I mean
manual work, physical work and how people could spend their whole
lives doing it.'

Initially Tony worked on the surface, separating rock from coal as it
came by on 'fantastically noisy mechanical belts', working with up to
30 men in a screening shed. The job was tough, filthy, noisy and 'very
monotonous, the sight of people doing it day in day out for the whole
of their working lives was quite shattering.' To break the monotony he
used to whistle, something that led to an unlikely friendship. One of
the young men standing next to him asked Tony what he was
whistling and when told it was the 'Emperor Concerto', asked where
he could hear it properly. Tony lent him a record and the friendship
went on from there: 'This set up of two young lads, one from a prissy
background, the other from a working-class background, swapping
bits of poetry and music is something I've never forgotten, stopped me
getting any ideas about there being something special about getting a
middle-class education … to be able to meet people like that … in some
senses better educated was only one of the eye-opening things that
happened to me.'

After about eight months Tony was transferred to work
underground. Bradford was a deep pit with little ventilation and was
tremendously hot. He worked eight-hour shifts following an
experienced collier; as the collier dug out coal, Tony shovelled it back
and loaded the trucks that trundled along the underground road. It
was hard, dangerous work. The roof was low and in places it was
impossible to stand up. After about ten months, he was involved in an
accident. Ignoring safety regulations, as many of the miners did, Tony

was bending down between two tubs of coal, when three or four other tubs, also full of coal, came down the incline and crashed into the tubs that he was between. As a result he left mining 'on a stretcher', with several broken ribs and a dislocated shoulder.

Life changing
Tony Parker was the only CO working in the pit and was looked upon 'as a rather strange being from another world'. Even so, he felt that despite his different circumstances, the other men seemed to understand his stand. 'The only incident of any kind was when one of the young boys came up to me in the bath one day and he said, "You're a fucking conchie aren't you?" and I said "Yes, that's right," and he hit me. That's the only thing I recall. Everybody else showed no hostility. Quite a lot of the older men were very sympathetic, particularly those I worked with underground.'

As a result of the accident, Tony Parker was no longer able to work in the mines but, still under the direction of the Ministry of Labour, was told he should do market gardening and went off to see a market gardener who employed conscientious objectors. The meeting was not a success: the employer asked Tony if he believed in 'the Lord Jesus Christ Thy Saviour' and on hearing that Tony did not, refused to employ him. On informing the man from the Ministry that, because of his lack of faith, he clearly did not have the right qualifications for the job, Tony was told he would be sent somewhere else. Nothing happened and in about 1943 Tony went back to his work in the bookshop.

For Tony Parker, as for many other conscientious objectors, who found themselves in previously unknown areas of work, being in the mines changed his life. In an interview recorded with the Imperial War Museum in 1986, he said his time in the mines was a 'turning point': 'I was very anti-war through my reading but I was nothing like as a radical a socialist as I became after talking with those old miners who had been in the mines for the whole of their working lives and would talk about the lock-outs in the 30s and so on and that really made me politically aware which I hadn't been before.' After the war, Tony Parker worked in publishing and went on to write plays for radio. He was actively involved in campaigning against pit closures during the 1984–85 miners' strike.

Hospitals and civil defence

Conscientious objectors were also directed into hospitals, where they worked as orderlies, porters, cleaners or ambulance drivers. It was often exhausting and dirty work and objectors were not always welcomed. Leslie Hardie worked as a medical orderly in a London hospital: 'For three weeks, we had a lot of hostility from the military patients: "I don't want bloody conchies touching me!" There was deliberate harassment: bottles would be poured onto the floor, trays tipped over ... We were told not to react to it, just get on with the job.' By contrast actor Donald Swann, who worked as a medical orderly in Orpington Hospital, found that the elderly patients he was mixing with had no antagonism towards him: 'I remember vividly bathing chronics – the very sick, old men ... They couldn't move and you had to lift them out of their nightshirts and put them naked into a trolley and take them to the bath ... They didn't worry that we were COs ... they were glad that there were men around who could produce a bed pan or whatever it was and they'd got us to talk to.'

Civil defence covered a range of various types of work including first aid, casualty and ambulance work; fire watching with the auxiliary fire services; air raid warden duties and police work. In the early part of the war it was organised on a voluntary basis but in March 1941 Ernest Bevin, Minister of Labour and National Service, introduced the second National Service Bill to the House of Commons. Among other things it made civil defence compulsory, both for men who were liable for military service and for conscientious objectors, who had been exempted from military service conditional on doing civilian work.

Not surprisingly this move caused something of a stir among COs and their supporters. Pacifist MP John McGovern condemned the Bill as 'a thoroughly bad measure in its intended effect upon conscientious objectors'. He outlined the position of COs who had been quite happy to take work on the land or in forestry, but who would refuse to do civil defence work because 'they would then become part of the machinery of war'. McGovern and others, also pointed out that conscientious objectors would object to being compelled to do what many of them were already doing in a voluntary capacity, an argument that did not carry much weight with Bevin. COs were highly unlikely to choose or be directed into the police service not least because the police occasionally carried arms. Yet he saw no reason why they should not be directed into other areas of civil defence, which he argued was a civilian and humanitarian service not a military one. The Bill became law and tribunals accordingly added civil defence to the areas that conditionally exempted COs could be directed into.

Conscientious objectors themselves had mixed feelings about doing civil defence duties. As McGovern had argued, some certainly felt that it was too closely linked to the military machine and while they were prepared to do farming, for instance, they were not prepared to do air warden duties or fire watching. Others, especially the more libertarian-minded, were prepared to do these activities on a voluntary basis, but would not accept compulsion, particularly when it came to fire watching. Another problem, particularly when the bill first became law was that some organisations, including the auxiliary fire service and St John's Ambulance Corps, were not too happy about using objectors anyway, although following government persuasion they were forced to change.

Many conscientious objectors were prepared to take up civil defence duties, however, and were not concerned about compulsion. William Elliot's view was that if a bombed house was on fire, then it was only humane to pick up a fire hose: 'if there's a fire, it needs to be put out. I couldn't understand the logic of those who refused to do it … except of course they would do it but not be told to … the country was at war … fires were breaking out, they had to be put out as quickly as possible.' He thought similarly about ARP: 'I don't think I liked it happening before the war because it seemed to anticipate a certain inevitability but once war had broken out … I thought it was only right that people should be provided with such shelter as was possible. Once war had begun fire watching and ARP were things that had to done.'

Many COs were prosecuted for refusing to do civil defence service but thousands did the work willingly – and received recognition for it. On 9 December 1943 Bevin speaking in the House of Commons acknowledged the contribution of COs saying: 'There are thousands of cases in which Conscientious Objectors, although they have refused to take up arms, have shown as much courage as anyone else in Civil Defence and in other walks of life.'

Community service
Conscientious objectors who took an absolutist stance were not prepared to take part in any activity that they saw as contributing to

the war effort. Some suffered as a result, being unable to find work and often leading fairly isolated lives. Sticking to an absolutist position in a social climate where everyone was being urged to do his or her bit for the war effort was difficult. With this in mind, there were many conscientious objectors who saw civilian work as a way of giving service. They were determined to take no part in killing but were keen to help ameliorate the devastating effects of the war on ordinary citizens. Giving service to others was an integral part of their pacifism and they welcomed the opportunity to work in hospitals, air raid shelters and with the poor and unemployed.

This was particularly the case during the devastating period of the Blitz between September 1940 and May 1941, when London, Liverpool, Hull, Birmingham and other major cities were heavily bombed, resulting in the deaths of more than 43,000 civilians, at least 139,000 injured and thousands made homeless. During the First World War, non-absolutists were known as 'alternativists', which sometimes implied that they had compromised their principles. The term was less frequently used in the Second World War: many COs preferred to refer to 'civilian service' or 'humanitarian work'.

Given employers' reluctance to use objectors, various pacifist organisations, like the Christian Pacifist Forestry and Land Units (CFLU), were formed to help objectors find employment. One was the Pacifist Service Bureau, which was set up by the PPU in 1939 to find work for unemployed conscientious objectors. There were also the Pacifist Service Units (PSU), which were created in 1940 by the FoR and PPU, to carry out humanitarian work in London and other cities.

Tony Gibson and his partner Betty were members of the Forward Movement, an anarchist group within the PPU. Tony served three prison sentences for refusing military service and subsequently worked as an ambulance driver. He also helped in air raid shelters: 'When raids started in September 1940 I did a bit of shelter work in Stepney and Poplar. I then heard of the Pacifist Service Unit to be told that I was *it*. Over the next three months we got three sections of ten going, which we dispersed around Chadwell [near Dagenham]. The main thing was going round the shelters in the mornings, taking the buckets of shit and throwing them down manholes ... in the afternoons we went to houses that had been bombed, rescuing people's possessions. We weren't much use at rescue work or fire fighting, but we were regarded as "good people". At the time of Dunkirk, when there was talk of "bloody conchies"; what are *they* doing?" our shelterers said, "Don't you *dare* talk about them" ... we felt ourselves needed.' Before going to prison, Tony Gibson had been earning a pittance as an artist's model; somewhat paradoxically for someone determined not to engage in combat, his portrait, dressed in an RAF uniform, was used to advertise Brylcream, a hair cream.

Before the war, David Jones, who was from a Welsh non-conformist family, had been a civil servant. When the time came, he registered as a conscientious objector, resigned from his job and volunteered to work with a PSU in Bristol. David found himself doing relief work during the bombing, taking food round to those in the air-raid shelters. The unit was based in the Children's Hospital, in Bristol, and he carried out fire watching for the hospital and for the Quaker Meeting House. Most were volunteers but David was one of four paid workers, although he received very little money. The unit also worked with young people in youth clubs whose activities had been disrupted by the war. COs most of the volunteers may have been, but workers at the youth clubs were very pleased to have their help.

When the Blitz ended there was less need for PSUs to help with relief work, so they increasingly focused on working with disadvantaged and vulnerable people, effectively doing social work. Units were set up in Liverpool, Manchester, London and Cardiff where pacifists and conscientious objectors worked with poor families, helping them to deal with financial and personal problems of poor housing, neglect, poverty and lack of education. Pacifists and sympathisers raised funds and based themselves in houses that they used as hostels and offices, workers going out from them to work with individual families.

Margaret Britten had been given conditional exemption to do social work and joined a PSU in Liverpool. She was the first woman in the unit and had to have a chaperone at first: 'It was family case work and the poverty was absolutely dreadful, there were children in the streets with no shoes ... they wouldn't go to school because they had no shoes. And the houses ... there was no furniture except a chair and a huge mattress on the floor ... the smell was ... outside loos, it was dreadful.' Margaret and others visited families, helped to decorate homes, assisted with budgeting – most of the families were deeply in debt – and getting children back to school. 'They loved us and we loved them. Very few people were aggressive to us ... in a way, they were a bit like us, they were ignored by the community.' Interestingly Margaret

Britten was not the only CO to compare her situation as an outsider with the situation of the socially disadvantaged.

The Pacifist Service Units eventually became a trailblazing model for post-war social work. Although very few of the workers had had previous experience in that field, their contribution during the war was widely recognised as excellent. In 1948 the PSU became the Family Service Unit and was one of the first organisations to develop modern social service. Margaret Britten and David Jones continued their work after the war and in 1960 David Jones was awarded an OBE for his work with the Family Service Unit, clearly demonstrating the valuable contribution that many COs made in the field of humanitarian work.

Hungerford Club

One humanitarian project set up by pacifists was the Hungerford Club, which was run by the Anglican Pacifist Fellowship (APF) for some of London's most deprived down-and-outs, who were not welcome in other air-raid shelters. The man who ran it was Bernard Nicholls, a Christian pacifist and member of the Fellowship of Reconciliation. His application for conscientious objector status had been dismissed and while waiting for his appeal tribunal, he started working with the APF and PSU running a shelter during the night and helping bombed out victims during the day. He was eventually asked to set up a shelter specifically for street dwellers, alcoholics and others who had difficulties in mixing with others. Backed by Westminster Council, the APF converted a railway arch under Charing Cross station into a very well-equipped shelter run by Bernard's team: 'It had a capacity of 200, 3-tiered bunks and a lovely fireplace that would have graced a country residence. The Council fitted up a marvellous canteen facility, a medical aid post and baths and lavatories. And thus we began the Hungerford Club. One of the most exclusive clubs in London – you couldn't get in without a special pass from the Westminster shelter service.'

Several of the men who came to the shelter were First World War veterans, and according to Bernard Nicholls 'were very interesting people. They were odd men out, contractors out of society, non-conformist, which in a very real sense we were too. Sometimes a few would get abusive and violent when we told them why we weren't fighting but nothing undermined the basic mutuality that existed between most of them and us.' One of the volunteers who was involved with Hungerford Club was Stella St John, a Christian pacifist, veterinary surgeon and conscientious objector, who had been active with the PPU before the war: 'It existed to cope with people who were too dirty, or too drunk for the public shelters, they were sleeping under the arches ... it was welcomed by Westminster City Council and Bernard Nicholls was put in charge ... he went along the arches and got to know people, spent the night with them, some of them were very nervous and wouldn't have come unless they knew him ... I did the canteen and ultimately took on the women, took on the de-lousing of the hair and clothing ... played games with them, we had a games night once a week ... with darts matches and whist drives ... it was all Christian pacifists on the staff.'

In addition to her involvement with the Hungerford Club, Stella St John was working with the Fellowship of Reconciliation (FoR) and doing voluntary fire watching and ambulance work. Later her refusal to be directed into other work led to a spell in prison. She was not the only person doing pacifist humanitarian work to be sent to prison. According to Denis Hayes, at least nine COs working with the PSU were prosecuted for refusing to be directed into other work; five of them did prison sentences varying from one month to a year.

Pacifist guinea pigs

One of the more unusual ways in which conscientious objectors gave service was to volunteer to be human guinea pigs for medical research being carried out by biologist Dr Kenneth Mellanby in Sheffield. As a biologist Mellanby was in a reserved occupation and not liable for conscription. At the time scabies, an excruciatingly irritating disease caused by the itch mite, which burrows under the skin, was spreading rapidly among the military and he wanted to study its transmission, treatment and prevention. Scabies, though very uncomfortable, is not life threatening and Mellanby, who wanted to use human guinea pigs, came up with the idea of calling on conscientious objectors for his research: 'The idea of using Conscientious Objectors had been growing in my mind ... I knew that there were many individuals who felt that they could not take part in the war as combatants and who at the same time wished to serve humanity.'

Slightly to Mellanby's surprise the Ministry of Health approved and he approached various pacifist organisations, including the Pacifist Service Units (PSU).

A residential Victorian house in Sheffield was adapted for the project's needs and in January 1941 the first conscientious objectors arrived. Over the course of the next three years, between 30 and 40 conscientious objectors volunteered to be human guinea pigs – Mellanby called them 'pacifist guinea pigs'. They were a fairly mixed bunch, including a maths teacher, a hairdresser, an artist, an electrician and various others. All were conscientious objectors and all were volunteers; tribunals did not direct COs into this work. Eric Farley was one of the volunteers and joined the project after serving time in Lewes prison. According to his daughter Susannah: 'My father did all sorts of things after coming out of prison … he volunteered to be a human guinea pig in Sheffield and went there for about six months. They were researching scabies in the armed forces … and had scabies introduced into their bedding and bodies.' After a few months though Eric Farley felt the research was becoming too militaristic and left to join the farming community at Holton-cum-Beckering.

Others stayed for longer. Bernard Hicken was a conscientious objector, who was directed into land work. Despite his firmly held anti-war beliefs, he felt guilty that he was living as a civilian while others of his age were facing death abroad and wanted to do more than just farming even though he was helping to produce food. 'I read in the *Reynolds News* about the CO who was actually acting as a human guinea pig in Sheffield for the Medical Research Council experiment and I thought this was something I would like to do because it's humanitarian, it's helping people … This was an opportunity to do my little bit in a more positive way.' He volunteered for the research project: 'We had scabies mites introduced into our bodies and then allowed to multiply and that was unpleasant, not too bad in the day time but when you got into bed at night and became warm then the mites became active and you'd spend a lot of the night scratching.' Conscientious objectors were also involved in Mellanby's investigations into lice, the 'shipwreck diet', which involved finding out how long a person could remain healthy on lifeboat provisions and scarce water, and Vitamin A deficiency. Bernard Hicken spent 18 months on a vitamin A deficient diet. He did not feel ill while he was on the diet but 'after eighteen months … I suppose nature caught up with me and I had to be taken into hospital and given massive doses of Vitamin A and I was six weeks in hospital with pleural effusion … that was the end of my experience of experiments … I was just like an old man.'

Thanks to the work of the conscientious objectors on the scabies project, Mellanby was able to overturn a number of widely held myths and confirmed that scabies needed warmth, not dirt, to incubate. He published a book about the project called *Human Guinea Pigs* in which he said that as a non-pacifist, all he knew about conscientious objectors before the project was what he had read in biased newspaper accounts, 'which made the men appear to be impossibly opinionated, pig-headedly obstinate and incurably ignorant' but that his 'illusions were soon shattered'. To his surprise they seemed 'both normal and intelligent,' even though they could talk forever − a frequent complaint about conscientious objectors − he stated that 'throughout the whole period of the long period through which they served as human guinea pigs − they co-operated in the experimental work with complete trustworthiness and loyalty.' Mellanby also mentioned the men's sense of humour: the project decided it needed a coat of arms and some of the volunteers suggested it should include 'a yellow streak, to draw attention to their pacifist leanings'. Finally though the heraldic device featured for the first time ever an image of *Sarcoptes*, the itch mite.

Friends Ambulance Unit

The Society of Friends (Quakers) has a long history of providing service to those in need and during the Second World War, Quaker groups and individuals continued that tradition both on the home front and abroad. Small Quaker relief groups began forming as soon as war began. In November 1940, they came together as the Friends War Victim Relief Committee and set up a training centre in Devonshire.

Roger Wilson, a conscientious objector who had been sacked from the BBC because of his views, was a leading light. He travelled around Britain setting up hostels for people made homeless in the Blitz, which were staffed by teams of conscientious objectors. One of them was Joyce Allen, who worked in a hostel in Liverpool: 'When I started at the FSC the fleas came out to meet me! They always got onto a new arrival. They'd been picked up in the baggy trousers of these young chaps going round the houses, and started colonies in the hostel. We tried everything. Sometimes we'd look at the children and see their flesh covered with pin-pricks; they'd been bitten so often they'd stopped coming out in spots ... We tried to get the children to school, we got grants for people in real need, we sent mothers who weren't coping to a sort of home for mothers and children, all sorts of social work like that.'

One of the best-known organisations and one that did a great deal to raise a positive profile of conscientious objectors was the Friends Ambulance Unit (FAU). As its name suggests, it was started by the Quakers and was originally formed during the First World War, when its members worked on ambulance convoys and ambulance trains with the French and British armies. It was disbanded in 1919 but with the return of a second global conflict a number of Quakers including Paul Cadbury, who had served with the FAU during the First World War, decided that a new FAU should be formed. A training camp was established at Manor Farm, Birmingham and the first 60 recruits arrived in September 1939. They issued a statement of aims: 'We propose to train ourselves as an efficient Unit to undertake ambulance and relief work in areas under both civilian and military control, and so, by working as a pacifist and civilian body where the need is greatest, to demonstrate the efficacy of co-operating to build up a new world rather than fighting to destroy the old. While respecting the views of those pacifists who feel they cannot join an organisation such as our own, we feel concerned among the bitterness and conflicting ideologies of the present situation to build up a record of goodwill and positive service, hoping that this will help to keep uppermost in men's minds those values which are so often forgotten in war and immediately afterwards.'

According to A. Tegla Davies, who wrote the history of the FAU during World War Two, those who served with the FAU were 'ordinary men and ordinary women', who included bank clerks, actors, mechanics, teachers, students, carpenters, lawyers, salesmen and factory workers. They were young, nearer 20 than 30, and most were Quakers, although not all. Despite the reference to 'ordinary' they tended to be idealistic and thoughtful people, some of whom after the war went on to become high-profile figures. Among them were composer and entertainer Donald Swann, architect Laurie Baker, who spearheaded ecologically sustainable building, Michael Rowntree, later chairman of Oxfam, composer Sydney Carter, and Richard Symonds, who later worked with the United Nations. Another early member was filmmaker Stephen Peet, son of veteran conscientious objector Hubert Peet, who had served time in prison during the First World War. Their motives for joining varied. According to A. Tegla Davies, they 'were as mixed as motives often are ... an amalgam of the lofty and utilitarian, of worthy and unworthy, of altruistic and self-justifying.'

Although launched by Quakers, the FAU remained a 'private, unofficial initiative' independent of the Society of Friends. Tribunals could not direct COs to the FAU, although they usually looked kindly on applicants who wanted to work with the unit. Instead the only condition they could give was 'civil ambulance work or civil hospital work under civilian control'. Nor did a publicly expressed wish to work with the Unit guarantee acceptance: 5,000 objectors expressed interest in serving with the FAU but in the end only 1,300 men were accepted. Women were admitted in October 1940 and 97 served.

As a young boy Sydney Carter's romantic view of war was steadily undermined by various influences – books about the First World War, like *All Quiet on the Western Front*, deep spiritual beliefs, and meeting Quakers – and he came slowly towards pacifism. In 1939, despite still having misgivings, Sydney registered as a conscientious objector and appeared before a tribunal in Reading. Three objectors who appeared before him were dismissed and struck off the conscientious objectors, register and he assumed the same would happen to him: 'if they did that to me, I said, I'd go to prison rather than give in. Pride, if not my conscience, would demand it. I thought gloomily of Oscar Wilde and *Reading Gaol*; but it never came to that. The Tribunal said I could do what I wanted, which was to join the Friends' Ambulance Unit, for work that promised to be "arduous and dangerous". I had asked for absolute exemption, which I did not get. Was it worth appealing? My objection was so wobbly anyway ... that I thought it wise to get into the F.A.U. as soon as possible. The comradeship of other conchies on the field (bearing stretchers?) would help to keep me sane and calm my doubt.'

Members worked for pocket money and were trained in first aid, stretcher bearing and driving. Most had hoped to go abroad immediately, but during the period of the 'phoney war' and then the Blitz many worked in hospitals, air raid shelters and rest centres. Sydney Carter had done his training at Birmingham: 'By now the bombs had begun to fall in Birmingham. After Dunkirk, there was no longer the kind of battle line we had expected. The only front we could get to was the London dock area; so that is where we went to do relief work of one kind or another ... By day I worked as a dresser in the out-patients' department of the hospital; but night was when the action started, till daylight, when the All Clear sounded, you were really in a war. The fact that several million men, women, children, cats and dogs were in it too make it harder to feel you were a conchy hero, going where a coward feared to tread. Making my way from shelter to shelter with my pack of medical supplies, with flaming onions hanging in the sky and shrapnel falling, I was scared as hell.'

Sydney Carter went on to Orpington, where his grimmest memory was working with very elderly men – 'a dreadful reminder of the dustbin into which the old are shovelled in our society' – then back to London, working in rest centres, and on to Newcastle. Making a trip to Scotland he encountered hostility from a farmer who gave him a lift: 'I thumbed a passing car, and a farmer brusquely told me to hop in. He asked me if I was a soldier, and I told him, no. Why not? I told him. Then he left fly with both barrels. He was a fighter, he admired a fighter. I should be a fighter too. If I was not a fighter, I was not a man. "If you feel that way," I said, "would you rather I got out?" "No," he said, "you'll stay there where you are!" So on we went, whirling through the country lanes, with him attacking and me turning the other cheek. I could not be angry with him; it was almost a relief to hear it coming out at last. No girl ever gave me a white feather, but this time I got them by the bagful.' Subsequently Carter was sent to the Middle East and in 1944 to Greece with what his *Guardian* obituary (17 March 2004) described as a 'stimulating group of pacifists' that included Donald Swann.

As well as serving on the home front, FAU members literally saw action abroad – in Finland, Norway, Egypt, France, Italy, the Balkans,

Syria, Ethiopia, China, India and Burma. The FAU staffed field hospitals, drove ambulances, ferried medical supplies, treated the wounded – of all sides – and provided help and support for refugees and others made homeless by invading armies. They frequently worked alongside British and other Allied troops, sharing much the same conditions and dangers and, on occasion, being captured and becoming prisoners of war.

Michael Rowntree, who had helped to prepare the FAU's statement of aims, was one of the first to see action in an ambulance convoy sent by the FAU in 1940 to help the Finnish wounded and refugees, when Russia invaded Finland. He then joined an FAU unit in Cairo, which was attached to the Hadfield Spears hospital, a voluntary Anglo-French mobile hospital unit, founded by Lady Hadfield and Lady Spears, perhaps better known as the novelist Mary Borden. Many FAU members served with the unit, including women.

Martin Davies together with a friend Tom Owen served in Burma. In a piece that he wrote for the BBC People's War website, he asks how 'a couple of conchies came to be following two tommy-gun wielding US Army Majors through the monsoon jungle'. The answer was that he and his friend were with the FAU. Before the war Tom was an apprentice in an aircraft factory. On 1 January 1940 he joined 60 others at the FAU Birmingham training unit: 'The FAU was a civilian organisation set up by Quakers, so that young conscientious objectors could have a positive, constructive outlet for their energies, in line with their beliefs, and independent of the armed forces. All were totally convinced – mostly on Christian principles – of the futility of war and all were determined to take no part in one. We awaited instructions to go, not to fight, but to offer what relief we could to suffering in war.'

During the early months of the war, the period known as the 'phoney war', Martin remained in England, working in hospitals and running rest centres for bombed out Londoners. His mother died during the height of the air raids and not long afterwards he went abroad with the FAU: '10,000 miles away there was another war going on between China and Japan. Forty of us volunteered our services in that field of combat … Britain was not directly involved … but conditions were grim and medical help primitive and whether British, Chinese or Japanese, they belonged to the same human race as we did.' Davies and a colleague Stan Betterton tried to learn a little Chinese and also as much as possible about maintaining and servicing lorries, which stood them in good stead. In June 1941, Davies and another five members of the FAU set sail from Glasgow, eventually arriving in Rangoon, Burma at the mouth of the River Irawaddy. Their job was to ferry tracks and medical supplies: 'Northwards, up the Burma Road and over the mountains was the only way to get our trucks and supplies into China, the coastal towns being occupied by the Japanese. The first job for Stan and me was to assemble our 3-ton Chevrolet trucks from the quay where they had arrived from America and to prepare them and load them up with medical supplies for the 800-mile journey up the road, "over the Hump" ... It would be a gross understatement to say that it was an interesting road. From the tropical heat of Rangoon, it led us through near-desert in central Burma to Mandalay, then to mountainous Yunnan province in China ... stupendous views of vast areas of mountainside, striated with countless paddy fields ... then suddenly you looked down thousands of feet into the valleys of the Salween, then the Mekon.'

Martin Davies and Stan did the round trip about half a dozen times. By this time Pearl Harbour had been bombed and America had joined the war. Rangoon was about to fall. While a colleague made a dash to load up the last of the lorries, hoping to get them into China, Martin Davies and other FAU members were told to provide ambulance support for an American mobile medical team in Pyinmana, about 100 miles north of Rangoon, run by an American Baptist missionary, Doctor Gordon Seagrave. For Davies, it was 'exactly the sort of the work that the FAU should be doing'. Working with Burmese nurses, they treated Chinese casualties in a makeshift operating theatre, but with Japanese forces advancing, they were forced to move northwards, ferrying the wounded and setting up makeshift hospitals wherever they could, including a deserted Buddhist pagoda. In May 1942, with Burma about to fall to the Japanese, Martin Davies and FAU members, together with nurses, Doctor Seagrave, some Chinese, Indian and other soldiers and led by American general 'Vinegar Joe' Sitwell were forced to retreat out of Burma to India. This was a long, arduous and dangerous journey that involved travelling by river on makeshift rafts and dugout canoes and trekking on foot over mountains until they arrived in Assam. From there Davies went to China where he continued working with the FAU providing ambulance and medical services.

Some COs outside the FAU felt that it was not an appropriate place for COs, not least because members wore khaki uniforms and worked closely with the Allied armies. However, members of the FAU always stressed their role was civilian; they did not pick up arms, although one of Martin Davies's colleagues apparently commented that with Japanese forces close by, he was tempted to do so. They were conscientious objectors who wanted to provide a humanitarian service although many no doubt also wanted the excitement, danger and involvement that the work brought. In January 1948, the then *Manchester Guardian* reviewed Tegla Davies's history of the FAU commenting: 'The combatant abroad grew used to stumbling across small pacifist detachments in unexpected places and even those inclined to abhor the conscientious objector were often impressed by the integrity of the best members.'

Chapter 7

Non-Combatants

'The worst of both worlds.'

Denis Hayes

Just over 27,000 conscientious objectors found themselves directed into the army for non-combatant duties only. Some COs actually said they were prepared to go into the forces provided they did not have to take up arms. Jack Newnham, for instance, who appeared before his local tribunal on 18 March 1940, implied in his statement that he would do non-combatant service when he said he would serve in the Royal Army Medical Corps (RAMC), widely regarded as a non-fighting unit. Jack wrote: 'Since September 1938 the question of military service has been a great problem for me. As war became more imminent I realised my mind must be made up. I finally came to the conclusion that Military Service, in the general sense, is not compatible with my religious beliefs. I am willing to serve in the RAMC.'

Not all those who became non-combatant objectors had said they wanted to do so; in many cases that is what tribunals decided. Initially non-combatant objectors had their names removed from the register of conscientious objectors. However, from 1941 they were allowed to keep their names on the CO register, so they officially maintained CO status, even though they were in the army. After the tribunal the procedure was the same as for entry into the forces as a combatant: the objector was called for a medical examination and, if this was satisfactory, was in due course called up.

'Mealy-mouthed Pacifists'
Initially non-combatant opportunities within the army were limited. Strictly speaking there was only one truly non-combatant corps – the

Royal Army Chaplain's Corps and that was only available for ministers of religion. Other Corps, notably the Royal Army Medical Corps, the Royal Army Dental Corps, the Royal Army Pay Corps and the Royal Army Veterinary Corps were seen as performing non-combatant duties, but in theory could all be ordered to take up arms. Many objectors hoped to join the RAMC, not least because it offered the chance of doing humanitarian work and, like Jack Newnham, stated their willingness to do so. Some tribunals added a recommendation to that effect. They may genuinely have thought it would be an appropriate posting for COs, but some tribunals probably used it as a bribe to encourage applicants to accept a non-combatant role in the army. Either way, tribunals had absolutely no power to enforce the decision. The only ruling they could give was that the applicant 'was liable to be called up for the Armed Forces to be employed only in non-combatant duties'; it was up to the Army Council to decide where a non-combatant conscientious objector would be posted.

At the start of the war the official position was rather vague, which worried the CBCO and others. Pacifist Labour MP Cecil Wilson wrote to the War Office in January 1940 asking for clarification and received a rather vague reply saying that 'all units performed duties that were by their very nature non-combatant such as sanitary work, clerical work in hospitals and pay offices and so on', but there was no guarantee that the COs' right not to bear arms or be involved in any potentially combat situations would be upheld.

Nor, at the beginning of the war, did the RAMC particularly want conscientious objectors. Some members resented them, feeling that not only did they not have the necessary qualifications or experience but that the Corps would be tainted by association. In February 1940 a member of the RAMC wrote to his local newspaper, the *Berwick Advertiser*, claiming that all RAMC members were being dubbed 'conchies', while another volunteer in the RAMC wrote a complaining letter to the *Daily Dispatch* saying: 'It is galling to think that places which should be filled with men who have given their spare time in peace time to practise first aid work are taken by mealy-mouthed Pacifists who have done no voluntary work in this direction.'

In November 1940 the War Office stated that the Corps would no longer take conscientious objectors unless they had specialist qualifications. Some COs were bitterly disappointed but others, as well as the CBCO, queried whether it was an appropriate place for objectors, given the possibility of carrying weapons. Later on in the war though a number of non-combatant objectors were accepted by the RAMC, particularly to provide medical help abroad.

Non-Combatant Corps

In April 1940 a Non-Combatant Corps (NCC) was formed within the army specifically for conscientious objectors who had been registered by tribunals for non-combatant service. The Corps was divided into 14 companies and the Pioneer Corps, an ordinary army unit that specialised in heavy manual work and was not ordinarily involved directly in combatant duties. The Pioneer Corps provided training and all the officers and non-commissioned officers (NCOs) in the Non-Combatant Corps. COs in the NCC were effectively privates. They wore khaki uniforms and were subject to military rules and discipline but were not issued with weapons or given weapons training. Nearly 7,000 conscientious objectors served with the NCC. They included a wide range of individuals, such as publisher and writer Roland Gant, playwright Christopher Fry, and artist Jonah Jones, who had learned his craft with Eric Gill, also a conscientious objector.

Once called up, members of the NCC were posted to different companies around Britain. Londoner Ken Shaw joined No. 9 NCC Company at Ilfracombe in 1941. It was a bitterly cold day and he and his companions were met at the station by a Pioneer Corps corporal, put in a lorry and taken to the seafront where the army had requisitioned hotels. When they arrived they found the hotels had been stripped of everything, so they were sent down to the basement to find straw for bedding and given three blankets. The next day, 'we were actually pleased, despite all our conscientious objections, to put the army uniform on because it was warm'. The 200–300 new recruits were then marched onto the parade ground and 'they endeavoured in vain to get us to march in some sort of order. They did this for four or five days and it was called basic training.'

Sidney Renow was called up in June 1940 and was sent to No.2 Company NCC in Great Yarmouth. Neither Sidney nor his colleagues had any idea what they were going to be doing: 'we'd got the idea that we were going to be trained as stretcher bearers but nothing came of that. We did nothing but marching for several weeks which made me pretty fed up ... then they wanted some volunteers to do clerical work

... and we were sent to Hemsby holiday camp ... while we were there No. 3 company was formed and we were attached to it and after a few days we were all transferred to Scotland ... and the marching began again.'

The men of the NCC were put to a whole range of duties, much of which involved heavy manual work: hedging, ditching, limestone quarrying, road building, laying railway tracks, loading and unloading supplies. Many also provided rescue and reconstruction work during the Blitz. Other duties included fire watching and helping to build barracks and camps. Official instructions stressed that members of the NCC would not carry out duties that involved 'the handling of military material of an aggressive nature', but this was not always the case and there were duties that some COs refused to carry out.

In 1941 men protested when they discovered that a factory where they were fire watching was found to contain shell cases. On another occasion conscientious objectors engaged on demolition work in Coventry were ordered to clear up a factory that produced aircraft parts. They refused to do so on grounds of conscience. On both occasions the men were put on a charge and remanded for court-martial. However, either they were not found guilty, or their trials were postponed indefinitely. Similarly in December 1942 seven conscientious objectors were put on a charge for refusing to make a road for an ammunition dump; again they were remanded for court-martial but ultimately freed and put onto other work.

Refusing orders

Many objectors who were directed into the non-combatant corps were fairly appalled by what they found, not least the endless drilling, rules, regulations and what they considered to be mindless tasks. One conscientious objector thought life in the NCC was similar to being in an open prison; another that the objectors were effectively 'round pegs in square holes' and felt quite unsuited to army life. Some accepted their lot, however reluctantly, but a number were not prepared to co-operate with the army in any way whatsoever.

Arthur McMillan was a Christian pacifist and member of the Fellowship of Reconciliation. He registered as a conscientious objector in 1940 and appeared before the Fulham tribunal, prepared to do alternative civilian service such as land work. The tribunal dismissed his application and he appealed. Muriel McMillan (neé Smith), who was then his fiancée and herself a conscientious objector, thought 'that the tribunal didn't really have much idea, really didn't have much understanding of our position … I knew he was sincere and it was disappointing that the tribunal couldn't see it … I had the impression that the tribunal didn't really understand the basis of our pacifism.'

McMillan's appeal tribunal directed him into the army for non-combatant duties. While waiting to be called up he thought long and hard about what his conscience would allow him to do. He obeyed the command to report to the army because it was an order given by a civilian body, namely the tribunal, but from then on was determined to refuse, on grounds of conscience, all military orders, an action that would lead to court-martial and military prison. In early December 1940 he reported to the army at Dingle Vale, Liverpool, an army training camp that had a reputation for extreme brutality towards conscientious objectors. According to Muriel McMillan:

'Dingle Vale had a very bad reputation for its brutal treatment of COs but he faced it with equanimity, he knew he was doing what he believed to be right and he had faith that he would be given the strength to face whatever came. He found that there were a few others … also refusing to accept the army. He reported fairly late in the day so there were no orders to refuse until the next day. I think the first order he refused was to put on army uniform. After refusing several times, in the end he agreed to put it on under protest. He was then detained for court-martial in the guardroom. There were several others there with him but then a very strange thing happened. Ten days later for some reason, which we never fathomed, he was discharged from the army and sent home.' When I discussed this with Bill Hetherington, archivist at the PPU, he told me that Arthur would not have been discharged from the army; it was more likely that his commanding officer, uncertain what to do with him, just sent him home on indefinite leave.

Arthur McMillan contacted the War Office, but no reason was given for this unexpected turn of events and in February 1941 he was recalled and sent to an NCC training camp at Ifracombe, Devon. Once there he discovered that out of about 150 non-combatant objectors, he was the only one who was going to refuse orders. He described his feelings and the course of events in letters to Muriel: 'I felt very depressed today as I am still with all the others, about 50 on my floor, 50 above and 50 below. The officers and NCOs are all very friendly and decent but the trouble is that all the fellows here are going to do the work and with the considerate treatment they have all had they were in great spirits … It only increased my misery … it is terribly hard when one is the only one. It would be desperately easy to comply. All real militarism is excluded … it would be so easy to do the work, doing it in harmony with others instead of standing alone and wrecking what is a grand relationship.'

The day after his arrival, he refused orders: 'After breakfast we were due to parade at 8.15. I refused to do so … I refused to the sergeant major … The parade was to proceed to the Records Office to have documents taken … identity card, ration book etc. I told him I couldn't join the others and he just briefly said I had to have my documents taken and I had to give them the necessary particulars so, rightly or wrongly, I fell in and went to the Records Office. I gave them my particulars and received in return my soldier's identity card. Then we went to the quartermaster's store where we received our uniforms. I refused to put on the boots, so they bundled a couple of pairs in. I refused to try on a great coat, so they judged the size and gave me one. Then we got a steel helmet, respirator, anti-gas equipment etc. I brought all the lot back here. Then all the fellows changed, every man jack of them and I just sat around feeling miserable. The only one in civvies.'

Not surprisingly, the sergeant major and the padre attempted to undermine his decision: 'the sergeant major … asked me why I had not put on my uniform and I told him. He said I was a fool … and I no doubt supposed I was clever and looked upon myself as a hero. I said no but I tried to be a Christian. He took me across to the headquarters and into a room where the camp padre was. This chap had on an army uniform and a dog collar and for about 20 minutes told me I was a sinner: "You must not do differently from other people. Most people are doing God's will. There is no good choice open to us, only two evil ones: to leave our friends in the lurch and to turn a deaf ear to them or to fight the fight for God." Then he went on about the evils of Nazism … and said my duty to my country must come first in the present circumstance. I could not eat food convoyed by the navy and refuse to help … I was simply bubbling over to get in my point of view but he said freezingly "Wait a moment please until I have finished." And then at the end he said majestically, "Well just think over what I have said, I am sure you will agree with me." I was unable to get in a word … and felt I had simply been lectured in a childish sort of way.'

The sergeant major took McMillan into another room, where he expounded all the reasons for fighting the war, showed his medals, told him his son was going into the RAF and said he had done all he could to make McMillan happy and comfortable. He added that he was a Christian, went to church on Sundays and thought Hitler had to be stopped by force. He also told Arthur that he was the only one who had refused. Despite the pressure on him, Arthur McMillan respectfully told the sergeant major that his mind was made up and he continued to take his stand. As a result he was told that the sergeant had been given instructions to dress him in his uniform. He received some unexpected encouragement during the process.

'He [sergeant major] said he had given the sergeant instructions to dress me in my uniform unless I put it on myself. I said I would not ... he told the sergeant to dress me. I did not help him at all. He had to take off my clothes and fully dress me in the uniform, which he did with little assistance from me ... While he was dressing me I chatted to him in a very friendly manner. He was a Scot who had been in the Scots Guards for nine years and had been in India, Palestine etc. I said to him: "You must think we chaps are a lot of fools," and he replied, "Every man is entitled to his own opinion, that is what I say, you must do what you think is right." That bucked me up no end.'

Arthur McMillan continued refusing orders, commenting in a letter that at least half a dozen of 'the other chaps ... have come up to me and said, "Stick it out old chap, we agree with what you are doing but we haven't the courage to do it ourselves".' Arthur had agreed a code in case his letters were censored. The word 'darling' was key. If Arthur used the word five times, all was well. If he only used it once, then matters were serious and Muriel would need to contact the CBCO for help. For Arthur the situation never seems to have deteriorated to severe ill treatment, although on two occasions when he refused orders to march, he was physically manhandled and pushed along the road so was forced to move, but salved his conscience by walking rather than marching. One another occasion he told Muriel he had the impression he would have been beaten up for refusing orders had the arrival of a captain not prevented it. His impression was probably correct because other COs at Ilfracombe were beaten up.

To Arthur's surprise, it took quite a while before he was finally detained and brought to court-martial. He handed in a written statement, although he was not allowed to read it himself. Various members of his church provided references saying that they did not agree with his stand but confirmed his sincerity. Following his court-martial, he was sentenced to 28 days military detention, which he served in dreadful conditions in Hull Prison, which had been taken over by the military. On his release he was sent back to Ilfracombe and subsequently to an NCC camp near Shrewsbury. He continued to refuse orders and went through a second court-martial, and this time was sentenced to three months in a civil prison. By law this now meant that he was entitled to lodge a second appeal with an appeal tribunal, which he did. Finally Arthur received conditional exemption and was directed to work on the land.

Extreme brutality
Arthur McMillan was fortunate to have escaped severe brutality but there were others who were not so lucky. While it is certainly true that conscientious objectors in the army were not treated as badly as they had been in 1916-18 when sadism was virtually endemic, there were nevertheless instances of horrendous physical abuse so severe that they were taken up by the CBCO and discussed in Parliament. The most extreme instances of deliberate and organised cruelty against conscientious objectors occurred at Dingle Vale training camp in Liverpool and Ilfracombe training camp in Devon. In September and October 1940, largely as a result of letters smuggled out of Dingle Vale, the CBCO became aware that a number of non-combatant conscientious objectors who had refused to put on their uniforms or to obey any other orders were being beaten up, half-starved, kicked and having their heads shaved. They were being kept in cells and woken throughout the night to drill on the parade ground. Although refusal to obey orders should have led directly to a court-martial, the objectors were being kept isolated and subjected to consistent brutality.

Peter Thornton, a conscientious objector who had been employed as a clerk to a magistrate's office in Leeds before the war, managed to smuggle out a letter about a conscientious objector called Albert Foster, who: 'refused to work and was brutally assaulted in our presence and taken back to solitary confinement. We asked to see an officer but none was produced so we could not register any complaint. The sergeant who assaulted him ... is an ex-boxer.'

Another CO, Bernard Gibbs from Cardiff, wrote in a letter: 'About midnight I was aroused and taken out in my underclothing, with bare feet, and marched around the yard, being beaten and kicked as I went along. I was taken back to the Guard Room, my palliasse and blankets were taken away and I was left to sleep with one blanket on the cold stone floor. I was again aroused at 2 a.m. and 4 a.m., marched around with others and then left until 6 a.m. the following morning. I was taken to a "solitary" cell in darkness where I was given bread and water and one blanket.' Leslie Worth was also beaten up on several occasions, had a bucket of water thrown over him and marched back to the guardroom, receiving blows on the head at every step. He was subsequently taken out to drill with men who were armed with rifles, and butted in his back with the rifles as well as being kicked and hit in the face.

On 26 September 1940 five conscientious objectors were taken into a hut near a firing range and subjected to continuous abuse. One of them, Fred London, wrote: 'There were about ten sergeants and N.C.O.s and they kept us running and marching, mostly running round and round the hut for about an hour and a quarter. They also put some sandbags there, and as we ran we had to jump over them. All the time they were kicking us as we ran, and kicking our ankles if we could not lift our feet up high enough. Campling [one of the five COs] collapsed and said he would give in but they dipped his head in a bucket of water and he was pushed back into the line … they gave us about ten minutes break. Then back we went and had another spell of half an hour, during which time Gregory collapsed and was similarly treated. At the end of that time … we all said we would give in.'

The severity of the abuse increased and on 9 October 1940, when 11 conscientious objectors refused to go out on parade, they were taken off to the hut again and were told to march around; while they did so they were badly beaten. One of them, John Radford, wrote: 'At first we moved slowly but we were punched and slapped, kicked in the ankle and other places. Bill Jordan had two beautiful black eyes, noses were bleeding, chaps went down here and there, they were hoisted to their feet and kicked off again, bad cases were treated with a bucket of water. Towards the end there were five or six of us down at once … I have never seen anything like it before and never want to again. We were mostly finished off with a blow below the belt … then we were held up by the neck and the officer yelled at us: "Will you give in?" One by one we gave in.'

According to Leslie Worth, the captain present, a Captain F.K. Wright, encouraged the beatings. After about half an hour of this treatment, the conscientious objectors gave in, were made to say they would obey orders and were told they would be charged with mutiny, a very grave offence that carried the death penalty. In the event, and as the news of the abuse leaked out, there was no question of charging the objectors with mutiny and the 26 objectors who had suffered or witnessed the brutalities were quickly sent to another NCC company in South Wales. No doubt the army hoped the problem would go away but it did not.

'Major Marlow, prosecuting said ... the privates concerned were conscientious objectors who had been removed from the register and put in a non-combatant corps ... The soldiers were thrown around the room ... if any soldier stopped for a moment he was immediately struck and either kicked in the stomach, punched in the face, or pushed. This treatment went on for some 30 to 45 minutes ... As they collapsed they were taken by one of the N.C.O.s and either had their heads put into a bucket of water or a bucket of water thrown over them.' (*News Chronicle* 25 March 1941)

Within a week, sympathetic MPs had raised the matter in the House of Commons. Sir Edward Grigg, then Under Secretary of State for War, promised an urgent inquiry stating that 'it is the desire of the Army to treat Conscientious Objectors with scrupulous fairness'. A few days later, it was announced that a Court of Inquiry was being set up. Conscientious objectors gave evidence and matters dragged on for three months until, on 28 January 1941, Captain Margesson, Secretary of State for War, announced that the Inquiry's report had been received two months earlier and one officer and six NCOs were to be court-martialled. The report itself was not published.

Joe Brayshaw of the CBCO attended the court-martial, which took place in Liverpool and lasted for 10 days. Most of the sergeants denied the charges and some tried to distort evidence, in one instance claiming that an objector had drawn a bayonet. Their defence also launched personal attacks on conscientious objectors, bringing into play every prejudiced view. According to Denis Hayes, 'the trials were a pathetic travesty of justice'. Some of the sergeants were acquitted, two were sentenced to a 'severe reprimand' and Sergeant McPhail, the former boxer, was found guilty of two assaults and later reduced to the rank of corporal. Interestingly two of the objectors, despite the brutality they had experienced, refused to give evidence, their beliefs not allowing them to bear malice for what had happened. One of them was even court-martialled for refusing to do so and sent to prison. Writing about it later, Joe Brayshaw commented that he did not know 'that I should have the forgiving Christianity to do it, but if ever men turned the other cheek it was these two young men'.

The other serious instance of abuse occurred at Ilfracombe training centre in April 1941, when four conscientious objectors who refused to put on their uniforms were severely manhandled by a Sergeant Maloney. According to accounts reported in the *Ilfracombe Chronicle* on 16 May 1941, the four were beaten and kicked on the head and body and ordered to stand holding their arms out for about 20 minutes. One of those affected was Denis Waters, a member of the Church of England, who had joined the Peace Pledge Union and in due course registered as a conscientious objector. His tribunal registered him to join the army as a non-combatant. He refused his call up and was arrested and taken to his unit by the police.

Once Denis arrived at the camp at Ilfracombe, he and three others refused orders: 'Four of us wouldn't agree to do non-combatant duties. There was this sergeant, an ex-wrestler from the London docks, and he exercised every kind of pressure, including physical violence, to make us change our minds. One morning he beat four of us up. My instinctive reaction was one of rage: here was this man brutalising us and getting away with it. But I knew that if I lifted a finger against him, he'd have it his way. So, I didn't do anything. I accepted his blows. Then he went stomping off, and I heard him doing the same thing in the next room.'

Once again the conscientious objectors affected managed to get a letter out to the CBCO and the matter was raised in the House of Commons. Sergeant Maloney was court-martialled for ill treating conscientious objectors yet he was acquitted because no other officers were prepared to give evidence. Denis Waters's opinion was that 'if this is army justice they can stuff it'. The four conscientious objectors involved were also court-martialled for refusing to obey orders and had to serve time in military detention, where they were given the dirtiest and most humiliating jobs. Denis Waters served three terms of military imprisonment and was then sent to a civilian prison in Wandsworth. He was eventually given conditional exemption and directed to work on the land.

These incidents of extreme physical violence were not universal but there were tensions between objectors and the officers and NCOs of the Pioneer Corps. Many of the officers and NCOs from the Pioneer Corps, who had been seconded to the NCC, were semi-retired or veterans of the First World War and had no idea how to deal with the men before them. They had been instructed to handle non-combatant objectors with care, were warned that the COs might well refuse orders and were told in some cases to ask rather than order their men to carry out tasks. According to various accounts, some conscientious objectors had fairly good relations with the NCOs and officers. Arthur McMillan for instance writes of the decent behaviour he received particularly when he was stationed near Shrewsbury waiting for his second court-martial, and it is clear from his letters that the officers recognised Arthur's sincerity and responded in kind. However, some members of the Pioneer Corps deeply resented being seconded to companies consisting of conscientious objectors and so tensions, if not outright brutality, certainly developed.

As Denis Hayes observed, it was an unhappy situation all round; 'The way of the N.C.C. was no easy one: theirs was the worst of both worlds. To the army they were suspect, while many a pacifist eyebrow was raised at the mention of the N.C.C.' So, not only did members of the Pioneer Corps resent the conscientious objectors, but also COs suspected members of the NCC of colluding with the military, even though they were non-combatants.

Volunteering

Within the NCC some men tried to counter hostility by proving themselves in one way or another. Jack Newnham, who had mentioned the RAMC in his tribunal statement, was one of them. Born in 1916, he loved adventure and had not become a pacifist until he was in his late teens or early twenties. When he was at school he joined the Officers Training Corps (OTC) and, according to his daughter Jenny Foot would probably have enjoyed it. On leaving school he worked first for a shipping company in a London office and subsequently in an estate agent in Pinner.

Jack was closely involved with the Church and helped to run a church boys' club. As war approached he began to question the implications in relation to his Christian beliefs: 'when it came to it, when everyone was thinking about the war and he was thinking about conscription, he realised that although he had been in the OTC at school, he couldn't, it was against his principles to kill anyone.' As already described, he registered as a CO and in due course was directed into the army for non-combatant duties only. Despite being in the army, the fact that he was a conscientious objector displeased his father who apparently never accepted Jack's refusal to fight, and, according to the family, never sent his son a Christmas card again.

Despite his stated preference for the RAMC Jack Newnham was posted to a non-combatant unit where he carried out various duties, one of which was to build a gun emplacement, which he and his co-workers refused to do on grounds of conscience. Perhaps surprisingly their refusal was accepted and they were moved from that job.

Many non-combatant objectors found their duties boring and often futile and, as the war progressed, they took the opportunity to volunteer for other work, particularly where they felt they could make a humanitarian contribution. During the Blitz, non-combatant companies were based in cities like Bristol, Coventry, Cardiff and Liverpool, which were experiencing heavy bombing and many COs did voluntary rescue work as well as their normal duties. In January 1942 two NCC companies were officially employed at rescue work at Bermondsey; the Mayor formally thanked them for their help. At least two COs were awarded George Medals.

Jack Newnham was a keen volunteer. According to his son, Gwylim: 'Dad always used to tell me that when he first went in ... they, the "conchies" were given a hard time and they were marched, square bashed until they dropped, and you know, dealt with badly and there was a bit of despising going on ... and he very early came to the conclusion that the only way he was going to make his way through it, to survive, was to volunteer for anything that was offered. And that's what he did. Any volunteers that were wanted, he volunteered – short of anything to do with killing.'

One of the duties that Jack Newnham volunteered for was bomb disposal. According to his daughter, he was 'first called up to Liverpool and was attached to No 2 NCC. In 1941 they were clearing up in the city after the Blitz, then farming in Leicestershire, then bomb disposal training in Newark. First of all he was in No 15 Bomb Disposal Company, labouring and then driving. In 1942 he was in No 1 Bomb Disposal Company, doing construction and bomb disposal.' According to his son, 'Dad always said he was nowhere near the danger but obviously he was. He dug up bombs ... In the sense that he was nowhere near when the officer was defusing it, but I don't see how it can't be dangerous to dig up an unexploded bomb. But he always made very little of things like that.'

Another who worked in bomb disposal was James Bramwell: 'We were a section of the Royal Engineers stationed at Bedford made up entirely of conchies of various types ... I thought it a combatant service, can't think how we got in. It could be dangerous; many officers were blown up in bomb disposal. I helped dig out an ordinary 50-kilo bomb. I was in the hole when someone hit the bomb with a pick. We all rushed out. I was so impressed with the officer, the way he went down to defuse it with me peering down ... He was very calm ... I was frightened of it.'

As many as 465 conscientious objectors volunteered for bomb disposal and were attached to the Royal Engineers in order to carry out the work. In some ways it seems odd that conscientious objectors should have volunteered for this task, but interestingly the initial suggestion came from COs in the NCC and, after a slight delay, the War Office agreed. From personal accounts, it seems their reasons for volunteering included a wish to prove themselves, to get away from the drudgery of monotonous tasks in the army and also a sense of excitement and a wish to be involved in the war, without actually killing anyone. Their involvement also seems to demonstrate again how varied conscientious objectors were and how differently they drew their personal demarcation lines in terms of what they would and would not do. They were young and despite their pacifism, once war arrived many experienced the contradiction of wanting an active involvement while not being prepared to kill anyone.

Vic Newcombe also worked in bomb disposal: 'it was physically demanding, which I never shirked. In fact, all through the war there was a conflict between my physical urge to be aggressive and do something and the restraint of this urge by the straightjacket of my pacifism ... We were proud of what we were doing and identified with the army very clearly ... I don't think we behaved in any way dissimilar to the soldiers. The basic distinction was what we were likely at any stage to do – we never carried arms or paraded with them and were never put in a position to kill anybody.'

More than 600 non-combatant objectors also volunteered for 'smoke companies', laying smoke screens in Britain to counter enemy air attacks. Many of them were based in coastal areas. The CBCO and COs themselves became concerned that they were in fact helping to disguise plans for the Allied invasion, which would therefore be a combatant duty, although this was strongly denied by the Secretary of State for War in June 1944.

Parachute Field Ambulance
A fairly large number of non-combatant COs volunteered to serve with the Parachute Medical Services, as the Allied invasion of France came closer. It was dangerous work and the War Office had been unable to find enough volunteers so decided to admit conscientious objectors. These men would effectively go into action with the invading forces but their CO status would be guaranteed. Their role was medical – to treat and clear casualties. About 160 conscientious objectors transferred from the NCC into the Parachute Field Ambulances, specifically the 224 Parachute Field Ambulance, which was made up largely of conscientious objectors. Most had never seen action and many were parachuted into Normandy on D-Day when the Allied forces invaded France. Their role was to provide medical support and treat casualties, military and civilian. Some later served in the Ardennes Campaign of 1944–45 and were again part of the Allied airborne assault over the River Rhine in 1945. Many remained in Germany until the final surrender in May that year.

After his bomb disposal work, Jack Newnham volunteered to be a medical orderly with the Parachute Field Ambulances. He transferred to the RAMC and along the way gained the nickname 'I will Newnham'. According to his son, while Jack was doing parachute training, 'one of the guys had refused to jump. They went back into the barracks to get somebody else and shouted out what had happened and Dad shouted, "I will". He thought he might as well get it over and done with so he was called "I will Newnham".' Newnham did his parachute training at Ringway, then went on to train as a nursing orderly and joined the 224 Parachute Field Ambulance in December 1943.

The 3 June 1944 was Jack Newnham's twenty-eighth birthday. The next day he and his companions were told that the following day was D-Day minus one and on the fifth they had enforced rest, dressed and were taken to the aircraft. According to notes that Jack Newnham made for a talk that he gave after the war, they 'waddled to lorries and were taken to the aircraft. Parachutes were put on. There was a door exit and seats along each side. Twenty men to a plane. There were six planes for the Field Ambulance, aircrew and a despatcher. All very subdued. Plane set off. Great praying.'

Jack was parachuted into Normandy and then trekked through the surrounding countryside, working as a stretcher bearer. He also served with the 224 Parachute Field Ambulance on the Rhine and in Palestine in 1946. According to his son, Jack rarely talked about his own experiences but 'he used to talk about the Americans on the beaches with great respect because of the terrible time they had there and he would say that his time dropping into Normandy was nothing like as bad as the guys who came up the beaches had. He had terrific respect for combatant soldiers but then we also found out, when some of his army friends came to his funeral, that they actually had great respect for Dad.'

Others who joined the 224 Parachute Field Ambulance included C. Hardinge Pritchard, a Christian pacifist, who later wrote an account of his experiences: *In My Grave I am Not* (1998). A member of the Fellowship of Reconciliation, he had registered as a conscientious objector but, following a long discussion with his chaplain, decided he was prepared to serve as a non-combatant with the army so that he could help the wounded on the battlefield. He was posted to a NCC company, volunteered for bomb disposal with the Royal Engineers, and in 1943 volunteered for and was transferred to the RAMC and joined the 224 Parachute Field Ambulance. He was dropped into France on D-Day but captured within hours of arriving in France. Another who served with the 224 was writer and publisher Roland Gant, who wrote of his experiences in *How Like a Wilderness* (1946), a lively account of his various adventures in France, where he was captured and escaped many times, finishing the war in a Nazi stalag.

Conscientious objectors with the 224 Parachute Field Ambulance worked directly with the army, treating the wounded of both sides and, apart from not engaging in combat, experienced the same risks and dangers as the soldiers. Some lost their lives, and many were taken prisoner. As with the FAU, their involvement on the front line did much to change the public perception of COs, although many other conscientious objectors did not necessarily approve of their involvement. Denis Hayes himself considers that they were on what he calls 'the Right Wing of the [CO] Movement' because although they

Books such as Aldous Huxley's *Ends and Means* and Beverly Nichols' *Cry Havoc!* had a powerful influence on shaping the views of pacifists and conscientious objectors.

First produced by the Women's Co-operative Guild in 1933, as a statement against the increased militarism of Remembrance Day, the white poppy was not intended to be disrespectful of those who died in the First World War. Instead it was a challenge to continuing militarism. Since 1934 the Peace Pledge Union has promoted and distributed white poppies.

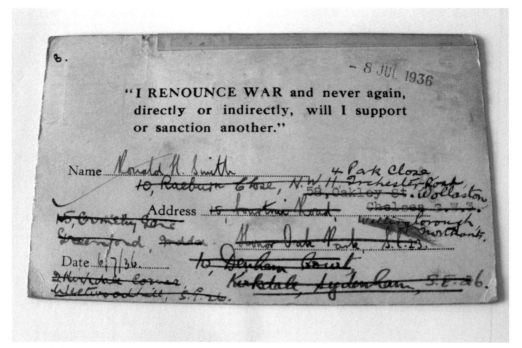

Peace Pledge Union (PPU) card, signed by Ronald Smith. All PPU members signed the pledge but, when war arrived, not all signatories became conscientious objectors.

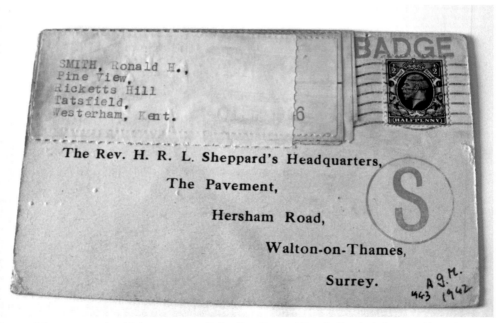

Front of the same card, which was sent to Brigadier-General Frank Crozier's home address because the Peace Pledge Union had not then established its own office. The stamp 'badge' indicates that the sender wanted a badge. *(Permission Peace Pledge Union)*

The slogan on the badge (left) comes from Dick Sheppard's 1935 book *We Say No*. The badge was produced by the Sheppard Peace Movement, which became the Peace Pledge Union. The PPU badge (right) dates from about 1937. It remained the badge of the PPU until the 1960s. *(Permission Dee Daly)*

Plaque to Vera Brittain, St Martins in the Field, London. Vera Brittain became a sponsor of the Peace Pledge Union in 1936, the same year that women were invited to become members. Vera Brttain's book *Testament of Youth* influenced pacifists.

The Peace Pledge Union issued this *Peace Service Handbook* to counteract the government's *National Service Appeal Handbook*, which the PPU saw as peacetime conscription by the backdoor.

In May 1939, men calling themselves the 'refuse-iliers' marched against the new Military Training Act, which effectively introduced limited peacetime conscription.

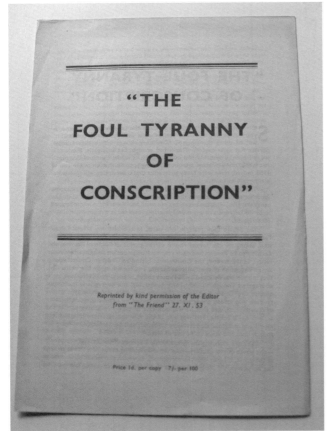

"THE
FOUL TYRANNY
OF
CONSCRIPTION"

Reprinted by kind permission of the Editor
from "The Friend" 27. XI. 53

Price 1d. per copy   7/- per 100

Quaker newspaper *The Friend* published this pamphlet arguing against conscription. Other peace organisations also produced pamphlets against conscription, war and militarism.

Eric Farley was a socialist and a pacifist. Before the war he worked as a clerk in the Treasury Department of Battersea Borough Council. In 1939, aged 20, he registered as a conscientious objector. His application was refused and subsequently he spent three months in Lewes Prison for refusing to put on his army uniform. *(Permission Susannah Farley Green)*

N. S. (ARMED FORCES) ACT

MILITARY TRAINING ACT, 1939

Certificate of Provisional Registration in Register of Conscientious Objectors

L.O. Prefix ~~WLB~~ WQ6 C.O. No 21/L 2150

THIS CERTIFICATE EXPIRES ON *Order by Local (Date). Tribunal*

Holder's Name.....*Farley E*

Home Address.....*20, Cromwell Road*
.....*Wimbledon SW19*

Date of Birth.....*24/9/19*

Holder's Signature.....*E. Farley.*

READ THIS CAREFULLY

Care should be taken not to lose this card but in the event of loss during the period of its validity application for a duplicate should be made to the nearest Ministry of Labour Office.

If you change your home address, etc., before the date shown above you must complete the space on the other side of this card and post the card at once. A new Provisional Registration Certificate will then be sent to you.

M.R. 61

Eric Farley's certificate of provisional registration as a conscientious objector. The first step to becoming a CO was to register at the local employment exchange. Having done this, the applicant was given a certificate stating he had been provisionally paced on the CO register. *(Permission Susannah Farley Green)*

L.O. Prefix Letters........WCB.

No..........21

BEFORE THIS FORM IS HANDED TO AN APPLICANT THE ADDRESS OF THE APPROPRIATE DIVISIONAL
OFFICE OF THE MINISTRY OF LABOUR AND NATIONAL SERVICE AND THE DATE OF THE LAST DAY OF
THE PRESCRIBED PERIOD MUST BE INSERTED IN DIRECTION (2) BELOW

NATIONAL SERVICE (ARMED FORCES) ACT, 1939

APPLICATION TO LOCAL TRIBUNAL BY A PERSON PROVISIONALLY REGISTERED IN THE REGISTER OF CONSCIENTIOUS OBJECTORS

For Official use.

Date of receipt of form.........3. Nov. 1939.

(If the form is received at a
Local Office the date of
receipt should be entered and
the form sent immediately to
the Divisional Office.)

Case No........London 2150

Cause List :—
Sheet No........36
Line No........6

Directions to Applicant :—

(1) The particulars asked for below must be given by the applicant.

(2) When completed, the application must be forwarded to the Divisional Office of the Ministry of Labour and National Service at ......59, Queens Gardens, Bayswater, W.2.......

The latest day for receipt of the application at the Divisional Office is....1.11.39........(date).

(1) Name in full........FARLEY, Eric.
(Surname first in BLOCK CAPITALS)

(2) Address in full...20, Cromwell Road, Wimbledon,
London, S.W.19.

......It is claimed that wars are fought for justice. But the outcome of all wars is
determined not by the degree of right on each side, but by the primitive law of
might. Wars engender increasing hatred and bitterness, intolerance and selfrighteousness.
Upon such evil forces as these depends the degree of justice in the peace terms imposed.

......The injustice of the peace terms arouses suspicion and mistrust, and a sense of
irreparable grievance. These emotions in their turn prepare the way for future wars.
The peace made at the end of a war is never permanent.

......War is a grand misdirection of the energy and courage of man; an abuse and
perversion of his intelligence, his patience, and his resource.

......War destroys the confidence between the common peoples of the world, raises a

All applicants for CO status produced a personal statement, which was read out at their tribunal. In his personal statement, shown here, Eric Farley stated that 'Wars engender hatred and bitterness...', which he profoundly believed. *(Permission Susannah Farley Green)*

Fred Vahey was an artist and a pacifist, who rejected capitalism and exploitation of land, animals and people. He registered as a conscientious objector and appeared before a tribunal in 1940. According to his daughter, Lorna, he was so irritated by the questioning, he just walked out. *(Permission Lorna Vahey)*

An absolutist, Fred Vahey was not prepared to compromise his pacifist principles and refused to undertake any war-related activities. *(Permission Lorna Vahey)*

BEFORE THIS FORM IS HANDED TO AN APPLICANT THE ADDRESS OF THE APPROPRIATE DIVISIONAL OFFICE OF THE MINISTRY OF LABOUR AND NATIONAL SERVICE AND THE DATE OF THE LAST DAY OF THE PRESCRIBED PERIOD MUST BE INSERTED IN DIRECTION (2) BELOW

NATIONAL SERVICE (ARMED FORCES) ACT, 1939

APPLICATION TO LOCAL TRIBUNAL BY A PERSON PROVISIONALLY REGISTERED IN THE REGISTER OF CONSCIENTIOUS OBJECTORS.

For Official use.

Date of receipt
of form........... 4 July 1940
(If the form is received at a
Local Office the date of
receipt should be entered and
the form sent immediately to
the Divisional Office.)
Case No........ S. 3640
Cause List :—
Sheet No.......... 100
Line No............ 5

Directions to Applicant :—

(1) The particulars asked for below must be given by the applicant.
(2) When completed, the application must be forwarded to :—
Divisional Office,
Ministry of Labour and National Service,

Park House, Upper Redlands Road,

Reading, Berks.

The latest day for receipt of the application at the Divisional Office is........ 6.7.1940 ....(date).

(1) Name in full........ VAHEY, Frederick
(Surname first in BLOCK CAPITALS)

(2) Address in full........ Innisfree, Pannel Lane, Pett,

Hastings, Sussex.

Any statement you wish to submit in support of your application should be made below :—

I refuse to be conscripted because it is a denial of individual liberty

I claim, as an individual, the right to act toward my fellow

individuals, & no less to all creation, in the manner that my intelligence

& my religious convictions guide me through the medium of my conscience.

Whatever maybe the reason for the universe, I see it as a whole

composed of subsidary parts & each part is again made up of smaller units

- infinitive.

The perfection of each whole is dependant on the wholeness of its

component parts.   The human race is dependant on its individuals & each

individual is, consciously or unconsciously part of the whole & his actions

should be such that he hinders not, nor exploits, nor harms in any way

other individuals.   His duty to his neighbour is obviously to do unto

him as he would like to be done unto.   If he acts contrary to this he will

be told so by his conscience.   A man may exploit, or even kill his

neighbour & drown his conscience in patriotic hysteria or some other

anodyne, but mankind does not end at national frontiers, so to kill a

Fred Vahey's personal statement, July 1940. *(Permission Lorna Vahey)*

This press photograph shows the first CO's tribunal to sit during the Second World War. Tribunal settings varied from being fairly informal, as here, to far more formal arrangements in magistrate and other courts. Tribunal members were tasked with testing the sincerity of a CO's conscience – an almost impossible task. *(Permission Peace Pledge Union)*

Tribunal members at a tribunal for women COs. Some 1,000 women appeared before tribunals during the Second World War, the first to do so being Joyce Allen. Both women and men experienced hostility and rudeness from some tribunals. *(Permission Peace Pledge Union)*

The Central Board for Conscientious Objectors (CBCO) and others provided support and advice for conscientious objectors. Some groups produced pamphlets, such as these, which included examples of questions that COs might face when appearing at their tribunals. COs were advised however not to learn answers by rote.

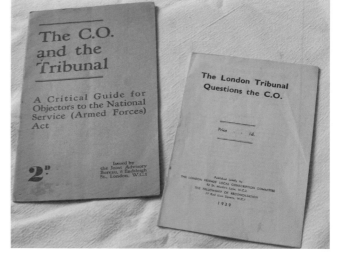

Conscientious objectors work with the Christian Pacifist Forestry and Land Units (CPFLU). The Rev Henry Carter set up the CPFLU to provide work on the land for COs. *(By kind permission of the Board of Trustees of the Fellowship of Reconciliation)*

CPFLU workers planting beech trees. *(By kind permission of the Board of Trustees of the Fellowship of Reconciliation)*

Workers with the CPFLU included COs who had been directed onto the land but were unable to find work because farmers would not employ them. *(By kind permission of the Board of Trustees of the Fellowship of Reconciliation)*

Fred Vahey using a horse and primitive plough on his smallholding during the war. More than 7,000 conscientious objectors, who were given conditional exemption by their tribunals, were directed into land work. It was back breaking labour and many found it extremely gruelling. *(Permission Lorna Vahey)*

Frank J. Stevens, an ambulance driver with the Friends Ambulance Unit (FAU). The FAU had existed during the First World War and was re-launched in 1939. A pacifist body, its aim was to provide ambulance and relief work', which it did in Britain and abroad. Although formed by Quakers, its members included pacifists of all faiths and none.

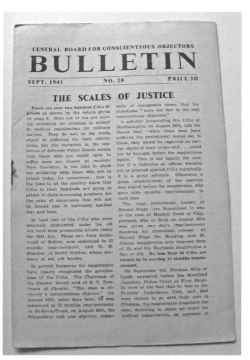

Article 'Scales of Justice' in the September 1941 CBCO's newspaper, *Bulletin*. By this time more than 200 conscientious objectors were in prison.

This CBCO pamphlet, *Court Martial Guide*, provided advice to COs in the army who refused orders on grounds of conscience and were subsequently court-martialled.

Three front covers of the *Bulletin*. Many issues included dramatic images by illustrator Arthur Wragg, socialist and conscientious objector, who was imprisoned during the Second World War. *(Permission for all images Peace Pledge Union)*

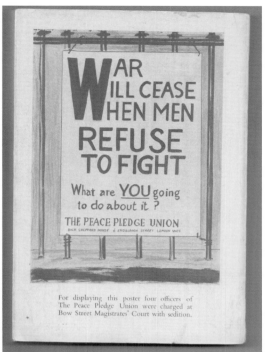

This is a drawing of a Wars Will Cease poster produced by the Peace Pledge Union. Its existence angered the authorities and in 1940 six PPU officers appeared in court, charged with attempting to cause 'disaffection' within the armed forces. The charges were dropped but the event reflected hardening attitudes towards pacifists and conscientious objectors from May 1940. The PPU often came under surveillance.

Fred and Zoe Vahey with their daughter Dilys at their smallholding in Pett, Sussex. Fred worked his smallholding throughout the war and was often harassed by members of the Home Guard for refusing to help with the war effort. Local people also regarded him with suspicion although eventually they accepted him. After the war, the family's self-sufficient and unconventional lifestyle attracted a lot of press attention. *(Permission Lorna Vahey)*

Michael Tippett, composer, conscientious objector, and president of the Peace Pledge Union from 1958 until his death in 1998, unveils a memorial to conscientious objectors in London's Tavistock Square. The stone was laid on International Conscientious Objectors Day, 15 May, 1994. *(Permission Peace Pledge Union)*

Detail from the memorial to conscientious objectors in Tavistock Square dedicated to 'all those who have established and are maintaining the right to refuse to kill'. Supporters of this right gather here on 15 May each year.

were undoubtedly doing humanitarian work, their actions could be seen as supporting offensive operations rather than opposing war.

This was a paradox that Vic Newcombe recognised: 'I was frightened. I was facing something new, and my first experience of going abroad was going into a battle of some kind. I could see the contradiction within it and could reflect on the transition from somebody who had persuaded himself that he wasn't going to take part in any single act that was directly connected with the war into somebody who was involved in what was a spearhead operation.'

Despite the paradox, the men of the 224 Parachute Field Ambulance were recognised as extremely courageous. When a commemorative plaque was unveiled in Normandy, the Brigadier overseeing events paid tribute to them, saying they 'were all conscientious objectors who would not bear arms but they would fight for their country and they all became stretcher bearers and medics. They went right into the battle and brought in bodies and wounded, British and German.'

'Mad' COs

On 25 June 1944 the *Sunday Graphic* carried a very odd story by their war correspondent, Leonard Mosley, who had jumped with the first parachutists into Normandy. He met a Nazi officer sitting in one of the Allied dressing stations near Caen, who said he had been told the English were mad but now he knew it for sure. Apparently the officer had been with his company on D-Day when the British parachutists arrived. He started firing at a British paratrooper but missed; the paratrooper dodged behind a tree and, instead of firing back, called out in German: 'Tell me, Herr Officer, have you any blankets I can borrow?' When the officer asked who he was and what 'this nonsense' was all about, the paratrooper said 'I'm a conscientious objector.' 'Then,' said the Nazi, 'Gott in Himmel, what are you doing here?' To which the CO paratrooper replied: 'Oh, our blankets dropped in the marsh and we've got some wounded men – a couple of Germans among them – in a cottage up the road and I'm looking around for something to keep them warm. Can you help me?'

Chapter 8

Refusing the Army

'He went away and left me trembling but quite certain that this was where I made my stand.'

Eric Farley

Tribunals dismissed about 27 per cent of those who applied for conscientious objector status. About half of those dismissed then appealed and had the decision overturned. Even allowing for this, about 18,000 conscientious objectors were taken off the CO register and made liable for call up into the armed forces, usually the army. Some accepted their lot reluctantly and went into the army without protest; others refused absolutely. The most effective way of doing so was quite simply not to turn up for the medical examination.

By contrast to the First World War, when the medical examination did not take place until after enlistment, the 1939 National Service (Armed Forces) Act laid down that no man could enter the army until he had undergone a medical examination; this was largely because so many unfit men had entered the army during the previous war. It was therefore illegal for a man to be called up unless he had been passed as fit by a medical examination. For conscientious objectors one way of avoiding the army, or at least delaying the process of call-up, was to refuse the medical examination. What actually happened to conscientious objectors who refused to submit to the medical was often quite inconsistent, so much so that the CBCO devoted a great deal of their time to lobbying the government and War Office for improvements.

At the start of the war the penalty for refusing a medical was a £5 fine or one month's imprisonment. Following the tribunal, what tended to happen was that a written notice would be sent to a conscientious objector, usually accompanied by a travel warrant, telling him to attend a medical examination at whatever place it might be. The objector either ignored the notice or sent it back, with a note explaining his conscientious grounds for refusal.

Other notices followed, some of them sent by registered post, but most objectors would continue to ignore them. In due course the objector would be arrested, appear at a magistrates court, and be fined. Some took the opportunity to make a public statement although this did not change the situation. The objector might then refuse to pay the fine and could be sentenced to imprisonment for varying periods of time, but at the start of the war 14–28 days was fairly common. However, the 1939 National Service (Armed Forces) Act also allowed for a man who refused the medical to be arrested and detained on remand in order to 'secure his attendance before a medical board or consultant examiner'. The period of detention was not defined and soon became known as 'indefinite detention'.

The first CO to fall foul of this was Charles Egersdorff, an art student and member of the Peace Pledge Union (PPU). His application for conscientious objector status was rejected, he refused to be medically examined and was fined £2, which he refused to pay. He was then sentenced to 14 days in Chelmsford Prison and an order was made that he be detained until he agreed to a medical examination. By July 1940 nine conscientious objectors were being detained in prison, under remand, until they submitted to a medical examination. The numbers increased and the COs' situation was highlighted in the press. The CBCO took up the issue and in August 1940, Cecil Wilson, a pacifist and Labour MP raised the matter in the House of Commons, asking the Attorney General, Sir Donald Somervell, under what statutory authorities courts of summary jurisdiction had recently imposed sentences of detention without limits. By October 1940 courts were being instructed to give fixed periods of detention.

Alexander Bryan was a 20-year-old student at Sheffield University. Brought up a Methodist, he signed the peace pledge not long before the war and also began attending Quaker meetings. He registered as a conscientious objector but perhaps because he had not been actively involved in many peace activities, Alexander's case was dismissed. He appealed and the appeal tribunal directed him into non-combatant duties in the army, something he was not prepared to accept: 'at the beginning of February the law finally caught up with me. I received a summons to appear in court for not submitting for medical examination as a first step to complying with the order of the Appellate Tribunal ... I pleaded guilty and was fined £5 and given a week in which to pay it. Failure to do so would mean a month's imprisonment, I was told. Then I was taken for medical examination, but I refused to undergo this. There was no attempt at coercion and I was then transported back to the police station ... and finally released.'

Bryan had no intention of paying the fine and on 7 March 1941, the day before his twenty-first birthday, he returned to his halls of residence to learn that there was someone waiting for him on urgent business: 'Even as I approached the steps to my corridor, I caught sight of my "visitor" ... he said "Well, have you got that money?" I shook my head and he continued: "Then you'll have to come along with me." I asked if he could wait until I'd had my lunch. "Sorry," was his reply. "I've waited long enough already. You'll get a meal down there." He was referring to the police station, for he was a plain clothes policeman ... I scribbled a hasty note for a friend, telling the news of my arrest, and dashed downstairs ... to my escort. Then we walked together to the nearest tram stop, talking as we went ... "I can't understand you blokes," said the policeman. "You all seem to know exactly what you are going to do next ... Who tells you what to say and do?" I told him that every pacifist was free to act according to the light as he saw it and there was no question of discipline from a higher authority.'

Alexander Bryan spent that night in a police cell prior to appearing at a magistrates court the next day: 'When my turn came to appear before the magistrates I declared my guilt and re-stated my refusal to pay the fine. "Is there anything you want to say?" I was asked. "No thank you," I replied, "Twenty eight days imprisonment," said the chairman ... At two o'clock, along with another prisoner, I was ushered into a Black Maria and taken to Strangeways Prison in Manchester. Once inside there, my clothes were taken from me, and after having a warm bath I received in exchange a complete but ill-fitting suit of grey and a painful pair of shoes, two sizes too small. Then I was provided with half a pint of cocoa and six ounces of bread.'

Stuart Smith registered as a conscientious objector in 1940 and when he appeared before his tribunal in October that year, he put forward three reasons for his conscientious objection: 'I believed wars could be ended, and could only be ended, by men refusing to fight in them ...

Second, I believed that if a war were fought, the countries fighting it did not have the right to conscript their citizens ... The third reason was that I regarded war as morally wrong in itself.'

He was 'surprised but not dismayed' when the tribunal rejected his application. Six months later he went to an appeal tribunal but the result was the same; his name was taken off the CO register and put on the military register: 'Some time after this notices began to arrive summoning me to a medical examination. About these I did nothing, being sure that I was not going into the Army at any price.' He thought about trying to join the Merchant Navy, with the aim of getting to a foreign neutral port and not returning. He grew a beard and got to Liverpool but ran out of money and returned to London where, a few months later, he was summonsed for not attending the medical examination, appeared at a magistrate's court and sentenced to six months imprisonment. He was sent to Wormwood Scrubs, where he served four months, with two months remission for good behaviour.

Cat and mouse

By 1941 so many objectors were refusing their medicals, and refusing to pay their fines that when the second National Service Act was passed in April 1941, the penalties were dramatically increased to a £100 fine or a maximum of two years imprisonment, or both. Many objectors were taken to medical boards under arrest, though force was never used on men who refused a medical. Ernest Bevin, Minister of Labour, commenting on record, said that he considered it to be 'repugnant'.

Conscientious objectors, the CBCO, and sympathetic MPs were still concerned about how many times objectors might be imprisoned for refusing their medical because one spell of imprisonment did not negate the offence. During the First World War conscientious objectors in the army were repeatedly court-martialled and arrested, sometimes as often as five or six times. The process of repeat sentences had been nicknamed 'cat and mouse' after the experiences of suffragettes before the First World War, when, like a cat playing with a mouse, the authorities imprisoned women, released them when they became weak, then re-arrested them and imprisoned them again for the same offence. It had caused a public outcry then, and did so again with objectors during the First World War. Many MPs in the House of Commons, some of them veteran conscientious objectors, remembered the situation only too well and when the 1939 Military Training Bill was being debated a number of them expressed anxiety that the same would happen again. Arthur Creech Jones MP, who had been a conscientious objector in the First World War, described his experiences to the House of Commons on 18 May 1939:

'I went before a court-martial and ... I was sentenced to a period of six months imprisonment with hard labour. I served my period and was then taken back to my regiment, given a military order, court-martialled afresh and sentenced to one year's hard labour. That sentence I also served. I was again taken back to my regiment, given another military order, refused to obey, was court-martialled again, and to go for two years' hard labour. I served the two years' hard labour and went back to my regiment for months after the war was over. I still refused to obey military orders and was sentenced to another period of two years' hard labour. It was recognised all through ... that I was a perfectly genuine person. Nevertheless I had been caught up in the military machine and the 'cat and mouse' arrangements began to operate.'

Partly as a result of this sort of evidence, an amendment was introduced into the National Service Act 1939, whereby a man who was sentenced to three or more months imprisonment for an offence committed on grounds of conscience, could apply to the Appeal Tribunal for a fresh hearing.

> **'Cat and mouse': First World War**
> During the First World War 655 conscientious objectors were court-martialled twice; 521 were court-martialled three times; 319 were court-martialled four times; 50 were court-martialled five times; and a courageous three were court-martialled six times.

By October 1941 nearly 400 conscientious objectors were in prison for refusing medical examinations. Sentences varied from one to 12 months. Neither the CBCO nor conscientious objectors knew what would happen to them once they were released: would they be re-imprisoned? One of the problems was that the law for objectors who refused medical examinations before going into the army was different from the law as it applied to men already in the army who refused orders on grounds of conscience. Under section 13 of the 1939 National Service (Armed Forces) Act, conscientious objectors in the army who refused orders could have their cases heard again by an appellate tribunal if they were sentenced by court-martial to imprisonment for three or more months. If the appellate tribunal then considered that the CO had refused the order on grounds on conscience, it could recommend discharge from the army and registration as a CO, conditionally or unconditionally.

The same opportunity of appeal did not apply to COs who refused medicals. As the CBCO wrote in a memo dated October 1941: 'Conscientious objectors who resist service in the Army are therefore entitled to have their cases reviewed after they have been imprisoned for their beliefs. This right forms a valuable safeguard against "cat and mouse" treatment. Over 300 of the C.O.s now in prison are there because they refused on grounds of conscience to be medically examined for the army. They believe medical examination to be solely for military service and the first step towards that service which their consciences forbid them to perform. Upon that they have made their stand. In no circumstances are C.O.s who resist medical examinations … entitled to have their consciences re-examined at any time.'

The CBCO decided to lobby the government to give these men the same rights as those in the army, so that 'their consciences could be re-examined by a tribunal as they would be if the men had been sentenced by court-martial, instead of their being penalised for the particular stand they had taken. Then there would be some end to the punishment imposed by the State.'

In December 1941 Minister of Labour Ernest Bevin recognised the problem, saying to the House of Commons that an objector might be 'subject to a sort of cat-and-mouse procedure. We have not yet exercised that procedure, but I think the House will agree that it is objectionable.' As a result, clause five in the 1941 National Service Act was amended so that objectors who refused the medical if they were imprisoned for three or more months gained the right to have their cases heard again before an appeal tribunal. If the appeal was successful, the objector was released from prison. In more than 1,000 cases appeals were successful and objectors were taken off the military register and registered conditionally or unconditionally.

Refusing orders in the army

Some conscientious objectors submitted to their medical examination but made their stand once they were in the army, by refusing to obey orders. About 1,000 of them were court-martialled and imprisoned. Eric Farley was one of them. His application for conscientious objector status had been rejected in January 1940 and he was placed on the military register. He appealed against the decision and in due course appeared before an appellate tribunal:

'By the time I appeared before the Appellate Tribunal in May [1940] events had begun to go disastrously in Europe. But I don't think that had any effect on the decision not to reverse the decision of the original tribunal. The tribunal this time consisted of laymen, the chairman being a distinguished historian. The proceedings were cool and objective. There was nothing fresh to be said, no new evidence so to speak. I cycled back to the office trying to get used to the idea of the unpleasantness to come if I persisted in my objection, which I was determined to do as far as I was able.'

Air raids were pounding London and Eric started making arrangements for his mother and sister to leave the city: 'I had received a notice requiring me to report at Kingston for an army medical, and had sent the customary explanation of why I was unable to comply. While we were in the middle of the arrangements to remove my mother and sister to the safety of Ilfracombe a summons arrived for me to appear at Kingston County Court for not complying with the medical notice.' At that time, the only way Eric could obtain a further appeal was to be in the army; if he refused to submit to the medical examination, he would be summonsed and fined: 'refusal to pay the £5 meant prison ... and after release a further summons would be served, refusal and prison following into infinity ... I had to make the choice of refusing or submitting; it was a no-go situation. With great misgivings then and with uncomfortable feelings of cowardice I appeared before the magistrates, paid my fine after using the dock for a further public statement of belief and submitted to the medical ... I was passed as fit for military service.'

On 31 December 1940 a plain clothes policeman arrived at his aunt's house, where he was staying, with a summons for him to appear at the magistrates court in Wimbledon the following morning. A friend from the PPU went with him and another friend gave him a copy of *Autobiography of a Super Tramp* by Welsh writer William Henry Davies, which 'would turn out to be a vital life-line especially in the first few days of confinement'. He was ordered to report for duty at the Royal Sussex Regiment but refused and was remanded in custody to wait for an escort to take him:

'By about 11 a.m. I was already lodged in the police cell. It was my first real experience of loss of liberty ... My life had to be made by me within that bleak space ... The wait seemed forever. No one came for me that day. The night was long and even W.H. Davies was unable to occupy the whole of my mind ... I can recall only one reasonable long conversation with a kindly copper who tried to put to me that were was nothing to be really scared about in army life.'

The following afternoon, Eric's escort, 'an elderly sergeant', arrived and took Eric by train to the Chichester Army Depot, where Eric was placed in the guardroom. He spent some time in the guardroom, in isolation, passing the time singing, and remembering poems, books, films and country walks that he had known. He was hauled before 'Major – who was very disagreeable and a little threatening' and visited in his cell by 'a courteous adjutant': on both 'encounters with authority I suppose I made it clear once more where I stood. (I must have seemed infuriatingly wrong-headed and arrogant.)' After these encounters, he was taken back to his cell where he sang and recited all the poems he could remember. He also spent time considering what his 'sticking point' would be:

'The definition of what I would and would not do came through practice. On the few and irregular occasions when I was asked (told?) to fetch food from the mess, I went, trudging through the snow, making my already grubby blue sports jacket still seedier ... I ate the food ... I shovelled the coke that kept me warm and went for a dental inspection ... and attended just one session of physical jerks ... I was very much aware that I was taking the easy route and my conscience was often uncomfortable, particularly on one occasion. I was engaged in cleaning the comfortable sergeants' mess ... a solitary pursuit which gave me plenty of time to worry about the rightness of it ... There was often opportunity for friendly persuasion from one or other of the NCOs present. One conversation in particular is memorable ... This very decent, quietly spoken regular corporal pointed out that my grammar school background, where, what is more, I had been in the Cadet Corps, made me potential officer material with a bright future in the army ... This clear, crisp image ... had a certain Beau Geste appeal but an image was all it remained.'

Eventually though 'the situation arrived that caused me the greatness uneasiness. I was taken by an NCO and a private soldier to the Quartermaster's stores to be issued with my kit, including uniform. Of course I showed no interest in this procedure and each item was dropped into my kitbag and a note made against my records. When this transaction had been completed and all the entries made, it was clear the private would be the packhorse, so I heaved the kitbag onto my shoulder, took it back to the cell and dumped it in a corner.' He was told several times to put on his uniform, the most threatening occasion being when a sergeant major 'returned from the pub late one night ... and swore and shouted threats at me through the cell door grille. This intimidation culminated in the dire promise that he would fetch other soldiers ... and forcibly dress me in the uniform. He went away and left me trembling but quite certain that this was where I made my stand. As long as I was wearing my seedy sports jacket and trousers and shabby brown shoes ... I was still a civilian.'

The sergeant major did not return: 'My extreme fear of physical force diminished progressively until it left me entirely. I knew I had won the crucial round.' Instead of the sergeant major, an adjutant arrived and, in the presence of witnesses, formally ordered Eric to put on his uniform: 'So there should be no misunderstanding the order was, I think, repeated twice more ... A few days afterwards I was put on company orders ... and stood once more before the Major. I listened anxiously as the charge was read out.' Fearing that he would be detained in the 'glasshouse'. Eric was relieved to hear that he would be facing a court-martial. He was moved out of isolation into the main guardroom, where he shared space with privates and corporals who had breached army discipline 'in more commonplace ways'.

Eric was also introduced 'to the prolific and exuberant use of ... "barrack-room language",' and received news from his mother and aunt of a fellow Wimbledon PPU member whose application for conscientious objection had been rejected and who had resisted call-up. 'He had also been taken to court and escorted to the Guards barracks at Caterham. The stress of the intimidation short of physical ill treatment he was subjected to there "persuaded" him to join up. Fellow pacifists were in no way critical of him but sad and concerned.'

In due course Eric's court-martial took place: 'I do not recollect much of the detail of the proceedings. There were three officers ... on the bench who ... were not on the staff at Chichester barracks. There was a prosecuting officer whose principal witness of the act of insubordination was the adjutant. I conducted my side of the story with Douglas [secretary Wimbledon PPU] a silent but strong support.' A few days later the verdict was announced: three months in a civil prison.

Military detention

Eric Farley was fortunate because being sentenced to three months in a civilian prison meant that he could apply for his case to be heard at an appeal tribunal. Others were less fortunate. The problem was that courts-martial were not obliged to impose three months, or to place offenders in civilian prisons. If a man were sentenced to even one day less than three months, or if he were placed in military detention, that is in barracks run by the military, the objector did not have the right to apply for his case to be heard at an appeal tribunal and the 'cat and mouse' procedure might kick in.

The first man to fall foul of this was Kenneth Makin, a Christadelphian, who had been ordered to take up non-combatant duties in the army. He agreed to the preliminary medical examination because he believed it was a civilian order and was sent notice to report to the RAMC at Dalkeith. He was sent a travel warrant and subsistence allowance but returned them with the words: 'I do not need the one and I have not earned the other.' During the night of 20 February 1940 he was arrested, remanded in custody and taken under escort to his unit, where he spent the night in the guardroom. The following day he was told to sign on but refused despite considerable pressure put on him. He was court-martialled and sentenced to 60 days in military detention so therefore had no right of appeal.

Sent to Barlinnie Prison, Kenneth was forcibly stripped and was told to put on his uniform, which he refused to do. Two sergeants grabbed him by the neck and hair and forcibly dressed him but he continued to remove his uniform. He was eventually left in his underwear for three days, put on bread and water and kept in solitary confinement. After nine days he was returned to his unit but was hospitalised in a state of nervous exhaustion and a chill that threatened to become pneumonia. His sentence had been reduced to 14 days. The case caused considerable publicity; ILP MP John McGovern, who had managed to interview Makin, raised the matter in the House of Commons on 16 April 1940. The Secretary of State for War denied all allegations of brutality saying 'At no time was any violence used for dressing or undressing.' Makin was court-martialled again but this time was sentenced to three months in a civil prison, which enabled him to appear before the Scottish Appellate Tribunal, which exempted him from military service on the condition that he worked on the land.

Arthur McMillan also fell foul of the loophole. While in an NCC unit at Ilfracombe, he refused various orders and was finally taken in front of a court-martial on 12 March 1941. According to Muriel McMillan: 'He wrote to me the day after it took place ... he was ... questioned to establish that his refusal was carried out in a polite way and that he had consistently refused to obey military orders. He handed in a written statement explaining his position. He had hoped to be able to make the statement himself but that was not allowed. He also handed in a resolution by the leaders of our church, which had been sent to him; they didn't all agree with him by any means but they were quite convinced of his sincerity ... After the court-martial he returned to his voluntary fatigue duties – mainly scrubbing tin plates – and awaited the result which was not given for several days. He was sentenced to 28 days military detention.'

Arthur was sent to Hull, where he was put into a military detention centre. The conditions and treatment were appalling. Interviewed by the Imperial War Museum in 1981, Muriel McMillan described what happened, taking her information from Arthur's letters to her: 'Three of them were taken up to Hull to serve their detention. Arthur was already in khaki, having been forcibly dressed, the other two had not been forcibly dressed and were still in civvies and they had a terrible time. When they arrived at Hull, in Arthur's words: "they do everything to make you feel small" ... You have to stand against the wall with your face against it at attention for about 10 minutes and you get filthy abuse if you try to relax, the warders are specially chosen for their brutal manner and their language is quite dreadful.

'Most of their orders, in fact all of their orders, are given in what he describes as "a hysterical scream" and the language is the worse he has ever heard and he assures me he has heard some bad language. What is worse for a person like him is that it is extremely blasphemous. The other two fellows ... were ordered to put on military uniform, they refused and were then beaten up quite dreadfully, they were lifted and thrown bodily at an iron gate and Arthur quite thought they were knocked insensible by it but they weren't and they continued to kick and punch them and it was all accompanied by the most dreadful screaming and yelling ... and this was only at the reception.'

Arthur escaped the brutality because he was already in uniform: 'They were put into the cells proper and his two friends were actually naked when they went up to the cells and for a long time during the first evening he could hear them being punched and generally beaten up. The next day they were in military uniform but he never had the opportunity of speaking to them to find out whether they put it on or they were forcibly dressed.'

Arthur was put in a cell with two others, which was 'extremely unpleasant' because the cells were not really meant for more than one person. The two men in the cells with him were not conscientious objectors. On rising, they had to wash, shave and tidy their cell within a few minutes, which caused difficulties if they were not finished in time. The hygiene was appalling: 'They are locked in the cells from four in the afternoon until six o'clock the next morning and have only one chamber pot between the three, which by the next morning is quite inadequate so the washing bowl also had to be used, without any time ... to clean it ... at certain times they were allowed to go to the lavatory but chances are just as you got there, you were sent back ... the conditions were distressing and revolting ... these were the conditions prevailing in military detention centres.'

Being in military detention meant that detainees were subject to military rules and regulations, with military NCOs in day-to-day charge of the detainees. The regime was rigorous and involved parading, marching, drilling and so on. Arthur wrote to Muriel that they had to keep their equipment clean, although there was little time to do it, buttons had to be polished twice a day: the punishment for not being well turned out was two days bread and water. 'On one or two occasions they tried to make the COs handle a rifle and took great pleasure in holding them up to ridicule before the rest of the detainees because of their refusal.'

Food was 'pretty horrible'. Breakfast consisted of 'some porridge, thin, cold and without any sugar ... in a filthy rusty basin with two slices of bread and a piece of marge that could hardly be seen ... also some cocoa, strong and unsweetened ... potatoes are cooked in their jackets ... the mud is not taken off, so it is all cooked together with the other vegetables ... meat was of the ... unpleasant gristly kind ... but there was trouble if you didn't eat it.'

No visitors were allowed and Arthur was allowed to receive only one letter. In terms of the effects on Arthur, Muriel said: 'I think it made him realise even more than before what an evil thing the army is, how the sort of values that one takes for granted simply go by the board under certain circumstances ... it went completely contrary to all his beliefs in the way life should be lived ... it stiffened his resolve, if it needed stiffening.'

Muriel told the CBCO about Arthur's experiences in detention, 'not because it was Arthur, not even because it was COs but because it seemed to me we were on a par with the Nazis and I'm quite sure that few people realised what was going on ... I was concerned something should be done about it ... for men whoever they were, they were men ... Arthur tells me in a later letter that the two who were beaten up with him at Hull felt it was not for them to complain, as COs they must take their punishment and bear witness.'

After serving his time, Arthur was returned to his NCC unit, which was now near Shrewsbury, and once again refused orders and was court-martialled again. This time he was sentenced to three months imprisonment in a civilian prison, where by comparison conditions were far better than in military detention. He had a cell to himself and was allowed books. He was able to appear before an appellate tribunal and given alternative service on the land.

Repeated imprisonments

Being sentenced to civilian imprisonment and getting the chance to have a case re-heard before an appeal tribunal did not necessarily ensure discharge from the army. Although never reaching the extremes of the First World War, quite a few conscientious objectors not only received repeat sentencing through courts-martial but also had their cases rejected by their second appeal tribunal and so suffered the whole experience again. Some of the worst cases concerned Jehovah's Witnesses, among them Bert Campbell, Gerald Henderson and Stanley Hilton, who were repeatedly court-martialled and detained or imprisoned.

Jehovah's Witnesses possibly encountered more discrimination than any other group of CO not least perhaps because of their stated neutrality in terms of human affairs and the fact that, although they were profoundly opposed to taking human life, their stated allegiance was to God before man. Both his local and appellate tribunal rejected Bert

Campbell's application for conscientious objector status and he was made liable for combatant service. Failing to comply, he was fined, arrested and imprisoned for failing to pay his fine, submitted to the medical examination under threat, arrested and taken to a training regiment near Ripon, where he refused orders and was court-martialled to serve one year's imprisonment. On 7 February 1941 the Scottish Appeal Tribunal rejected his appeal and he was sent back to his regiment.

Bert was again imprisoned for failing to obey orders and on 14 June 1941 his second court-martial, taking the view that if Campbell had already been rejected by the previous appeal he could not be a genuine conscientious objector, sentenced him to two years' detention. A Quaker observer described it as a 'very great miscarriage of justice'. Friends, the CBCO and others lobbied on his behalf and his sentence was remitted and Campbell was returned to his unit. He immediately disobeyed orders and was court-martialled a third time and sentenced to two years imprisonment, appearing before an appellate tribunal again on 28 April 1942. This time, a sympathetic tribunal registered him as a conscientious objector conditional on doing civilian work. He was discharged from the army on 15 May 1942, having served almost 20 months continuously in prison or detention.

The case of Stanley Hilton, a wood worker and Jehovah's Witness, was even more prolonged. Dismissed by his local and appeal tribunal, he was arrested on 2 September 1940 for being absent from a unit of the Royal Artillery. Like Campbell, he served one year in prison, but was rejected again by the appeal tribunal, followed by two years military detention, and two years imprisonment. However, unlike Campbell, his third appeal was also rejected and he was returned to prison, finally coming out in June 1943 and being returned to the army. He went through a fourth court-martial on 26 July 1943. Fenner Brockway, chair of the CBCO, provided a character witness but the court-martial sentenced Hilton to two years' detention and he was taken to Riddrie Detention Barracks, Glasgow. At this point there was a public outcry and the press, not always sympathetic to conscientious objectors, protested about the situation. The case was raised in Parliament, the CBCO organised a letter-writing campaign and published a pamphlet *The Case for Stanley Hilton*, and Fenner Brockway sent a letter of protest, which was printed in some 15 newspapers.

Initially there was little progress but in October Hilton's sentence was suspended. Within a couple of weeks however the 'cat and mouse' cycle began all over again. Hilton was posted to a local regiment where, refusing to comply, he found himself facing a fifth court-martial. By this time he was also physically unwell; his cell was freezing and he had flu. He was sentenced to twelve months imprisonment, which gave him the right to yet another appeal tribunal. Evidence of his sincerity was presented and he was finally registered as a conscientious objector, conditional on undertaking work underground in coal mining – a harsh decision. He refused to comply but no further action was taken. Hilton's case was the best known but not the only instance. More than 200 conscientious objectors were court-martialled twice and just over 100 three times. Fifteen men were court-martialled four times, two men five times and one man experienced six court-martials.

Chapter 9

Prison

'Prison has left a lifetime's impression on me ... if it had been any harder it would have broken me in health, in mind and body.'

Kathleen Wigham

As every conscientious objector knew, refusing on grounds of conscience to abide by the terms of a tribunal could lead to a prison sentence. There were fewer absolutists during the Second World War than in the First, possibly because tribunals offered a wider range of civilian work and perhaps too because it was such a different war. Most conscientious objectors were prepared to comply with the terms of their tribunals, provided they did not conflict with their conscience.

However, there were others who, on grounds of conscience, were not prepared to accept tribunal decisions and took a stand against them, even if prison was the logical outcome. This applied to refusal to undertake compulsory military service but also to industrial compulsion and being compelled to undertake civil defence duties, such as fire watching for incendiary bombs. Official attitudes were more tolerant to Second World War conscientious objectors than they had been 20 years previously and no doubt the government wanted to avoid turning conscientious objectors into martyrs by imposing the savage prison sentences of the First World War, but even so about 6,000 men and 500 women served time in prison during the Second World War on grounds of conscience. The reasons varied: while some refused to enter the army or obey orders in the army, others refused to do certain types of civilian work, and many of these were women.

Taking a stand that led to prison was a daunting prospect, but those who did so felt they had no other choice but to bear witness and take their conscientious stand as far as possible, no matter what the consequences. COs in prison were treated more leniently than in the First World War, though there were some instances of brutality and even for those who escaped physical violence, the mere act of going to prison could carry a long-lasting stigma. Most COs coped with prison but being locked away in unfamiliar and primitive conditions could take its toll.

Into Lewes Prison

Eric Farley was sent to Lewes Prison, in Sussex, to serve his three months. This was a far cry from his pre-war life working in local government: 'It was getting dark by the time I clambered into the open-backed army truck ... The escorting sergeant sat beside the driver. A private sat beside me and the passing world which I observed closely to imprint the scene on memory as one of my resources during the next months of enforced seclusion ... The dark ploughed land moved me greatly ... Having been deprived of it, I felt even more strongly that this was my country. It had always been part of the landscape of my mind.'

When Eric Farley arrived at the prison: 'A bell was rung, the door within the door for foot passengers opened ... My body was handed over and signed for ... I have a memory of being taken across a great yard towards impenetrable buildings ... The scene that ensued ... was almost familiar to me from fiction and films ... the undressing and handing over ... of clothing and possessions ... The atmosphere was bleak and impersonal, a feeling compounded as a warder bearing a bunch of huge keys shot locks, wrenched doors open and crashed them closed ... The tiled areas shook with intimidating metallic noise. The final clang as my cell door closed made my isolation complete. I had only the chill chamber pot for company and even that did not belong to me. The contrast with my recent intimacy with the open Sussex countryside was crushing.'

The following morning: 'The warder appeared on the doorway together with a prisoner who dished out porridge, a cob of greyish bread and a small slab of margarine, and a mug of sweet, milky tea. The first morning, I just could not swallow the porridge which had the appearance of stodgy hen seed. There were spiky ears of grain on the surface. Apprehension made for difficulty in swallowing anyway.' Later that day, Eric was transferred from the reception block to his cell on a first floor gallery and subsequently taken to the governor of the prison. His main concern was to find out how he could make an appeal to the tribunal: 'The governor, a courteous ex-naval commander, having first delivered a homily on good behaviour … was then open to requests. He knew of no specific procedure [for an appeal]. I was once more the first oddball of my particular kind he had been called upon to deal with.'

Eric 'moved through that first day like an animal sensing an alien habitat, forcing myself not to think beyond the moment. Before the rhythm of a complete 24 hours was known it was impossible to measure the physical and mental resources needed for its accomplishment.' Together with other first offenders, he was set to work sewing mailbags, which was one of the few times, apart from brief exercise periods, 'when we were allowed out into the blessed air,' that he saw other prisoners. He was locked into his cell at around four pm, had cocoa and 'a cob of bread' at five pm and remained in his cell until seven-thirty am the next morning. 'So there I was in that confined space with its cold, slippery walls, its window high up in the wall opposite the heavy metal door with its spy hole, through which an eye could observe me but which I could not look out of. But I could at least see the sky and, if I stood on my chair, the windows of other cell blocks across the yard. The only company I had in addition to my own, was an enamel dinner plate and mug, a tinny little knife, fork and spoon, all resting on a ledge set into one wall, with my enamel bowl on a ledge opposite and a corresponding bucket of water beneath, a large ledge with mattress and blankets serving as a bed. That left the Bible … and I began to read the gospels for the first time for many, many years.' Lights were switched off at nine pm. Eric 'hadn't spent so much time in bed since I was a child'.

As time passed, Eric got used to the prison regime; most prisoners were either first-timers or 'old lags' although there was one member of the IRA in the prison, who was regarded with some awe. After a while he was 'promoted' to landing orderly, which involved cleaning the landings, sweeping with a broom then getting down on hands and knees scrubbing and rinsing. He did not encounter any hostility from other prisoners for being a conscientious objector and by and large the authorities left him alone but 'the one real punishment I had to face on this privileged job each day … was cleaning out the W.C. after they had undergone their swamping use by far too many men'. Like many prisoners, Eric Farley wrote about the humiliation and indignity of slopping out overfull chamber pots each morning and writes in his memoirs that 'The first time I opened the half-door to discover the overflowing pan and the floor and lower walls slimed copiously with other people's shit and piss and sodden paper, my revulsion was so strong, I could have run except I knew I was expected to turn that obscene display into a place of chemical hygiene ... it was a necessary part of my education in overcoming repugnance to physical unpleasantness ... The great compensation for this nauseating task was the free use of the freshly-shone W.C.'

Eric was allowed to receive and send one letter a month. Given the restrictions, his friends and colleagues passed on news through his mother who wrote every month. He also received two visits, one from a Quaker prison visitor, which was the first time he was able to talk with someone who shared his views and another from a fellow CO, who was working with the Fire Service at Woolwich. Things looked up when he was transferred to working in the prison library. Another encouraging event was the arrival of an official form of appeal to a tribunal. By now he had decided to make a compromise: 'I had decided by this time that making a stand on principle would not stop the war, might even be a form of self-indulgence, and that the greater part of me was wasted in prison. I felt a great need to take part in the fuller life of all those people outside. I still felt the tug of absolutism though and admired and still admire those that follow that difficult road. But in the end I withdrew my plea for unconditional registration as a C.O. and asked for exemption from military service conditional on my agreeing to do social service. That was where my compromise stuck. I knew that I could never agree to military service even as a non-combatant.'

He was released from prison in early April 1941 and returned to Chichester barracks, where he was held in the guardroom for a week or so until being taken under escort to London for his appeal tribunal: 'There had been one of the heaviest air raids on London the night before ... There were hoses, water and broken glass everywhere.' At his tribunal, Eric was asked about the sources of his beliefs: 'If they did not come from religious conviction, how did I account for my moral beliefs ... I referred ... characteristically to literature, in particular *War and Peace* and Aldous Huxley's *Ends and Means*.' To his surprise and consternation, he was also asked why he had been selective about the activities he had chosen to do at Chichester, such as fetching food and shovelling coal to which he replied that that as he ate the food, he could not refuse to fetch it, that as he kept warm, he could not refuse to shovel coal but that he was a civilian member 'of that society with whose members as individuals, I shared much in common. What I did not share was their role as soldiers and ... made that distinction clear by refusing to put on army uniform.' Apprehensive about the result, he was escorted back to Chichester, and a few days later heard he had been given conditional exemption and was discharged from the army.

Coping with prison life

Stuart Smith had been sentenced to six months in Wormwood Scrubs. He found he was able to cope with prison and was not too bothered by the isolation: 'A period of four months (six months less remission of two) is not a long time unless something is acutely unpleasant – and nothing was. To have to sleep fully clothed because of the cold and to be thinking rather often about food ... are no great deprivations ... The weather turned warmer, and I was fortunate enough to get a job taking food around. Anyone lucky enough to get [this] job not only got as much as he could possibly eat but was also in a position to fiddle some extra food for his friends ... What seemed to be the greatest deprivation, and certainly was to many prisoners, a solitary confinement for about 18 hours a day, did not worry me.'

Wormwood Scrubs was used as a central prison for all conscientious objectors in London as well as a temporary holding prison for those waiting for appeal tribunals, so when Smith arrived he discovered there were about 200 other conscientious objectors there, 'some of whom were serving sentences double the length of mine and some of whom may have undergone real distress ... But my impression was that this was not so.'

While in prison, Smith discovered that if he chose to do so he could appear again before a tribunal and, if he agreed to land work or another form of civilian service, he would stand a good chance of being released immediately. He did not, however, take this option and when he was released, in May 1942, found a gardening job through a Quaker, John Fletcher, who had been an absolutist during the First World War. After a few months the Ministry of Labour contacted him and suggested that if he joined other conscientious objectors who were working for the local War Agricultural Committees, 'the authorities would be glad to let bygones be bygones'. Failure to do so might have led to further prison sentences so John exchanged gardening for land work and escaped any further attention from the authorities.

Jehovah's Witnesses

Some COs did experience hostility in prison, among them Jehovah's Witnesses. William Heard, a Jehovah's Witness, refused to take up non-combatant duties and was sent to Feltham Borstal, the young offenders' prison in May 1940. From the first night, he was bullied constantly, having a slop bucket thrown over him while he was in bed, and hot cocoa poured down his neck. He was also regularly beaten up and on one occasion had his teeth knocked out. In an interview with the Imperial War Museum in 1980, he described how the wardens just turned a blind eye.

Two or so years later, Douglas Beavor was also sent to Feltham. Born in 1924, his parents became Jehovah's Witnesses as did he when he was 14. Like all Jehovah's Witnesses, he was not prepared to fight and registered as a conscientious objector. In his view, tribunals rarely recognised Jehovah's Witnesses as genuine COs and he was dismissed and put on the military register. He refused to attend medical examinations and was eventually summonsed and sentenced to one year in Feltham: 'The court wasn't interested ... in our beliefs ... it was just "Did you take it [medical] or didn't you?" and if you said you didn't, well then you were guilty ... I think they thought "Well, you're taking a cowardly way out, you should be in the army" ... you deserved everything you got, that was their attitude.'

Douglas was sentenced to one year in prison and taken to Feltham Prison in a Black Maria. When he arrived he was put into a block of individual cells: 'at the Borstal most of the young prisoners live in communal living, maybe 100 in a dormitory ... Earlier prisoners, who were conscientious objectors and Jehovah's Witnesses were put into these wings but they had a really rough time from the inmates. They were teased and beaten and things got really violent at times. The prison authorities realised this wasn't a good thing and they decided to keep the ones who were there for matters of conscience in the individual cells.'

Probably as a result of segregating the young offenders, Douglas did not experience the same brutality as William Heard. Prison officers whom he had close contact with were quite understanding but he did encounter 'a very hostile attitude' whenever he came into contact with other young offenders. He had, however, been well briefed by his father Ernest, who advised him to 'keep a positive enthusiastic outlook' and 'to keep spiritually strong, to use the time in prison to get an accurate knowledge of the Bible'. Douglas believed it was good advice and his father would have known – Ernest Beavor served two years hard labour in Wormwood Scrubs for his conscientious stand, coming out of prison at much the same time as his son went in.

In or out of prison, Jehovah's Witnesses experienced probably more discrimination than other COs, so much so that in 1944 Dr Temple, then Archbishop of Canterbury and no pacifist, wrote to the Minister of Labour about Jehovah's Witnesses who, having refused medical examinations, had been imprisoned and subsequently offered civilian work that they refused: 'I have had sent to me a statement giving the position of the first 18 cases where prosecutions have been instituted for the third time ... nearly all these people are "Jehovah's Witnesses". I regard that group as particularly wrong-headed and vexatious but it is difficult to avoid the impression ... that there is a deliberate persecution of this group.' Ernest Bevin eventually replied, denying this was the case. Either way, evidence points to the fact that they were very badly treated.

Refusing civilian work

Quite a number of conscientious objectors were jailed for refusing to comply with their conditions of exemption: they had been conditionally exempted by tribunals provided they did certain types of civilian work but felt they could not, on grounds of conscience, take up the work. The reasons varied: some saw the work as too closely linked to militarism; others argued that by taking up the work they were freeing up another worker for conscription; and still others argued that the work they were already doing was more appropriate and often more useful. There was also the knotty question of civil defence duties – while some objectors were happy to do duties such as fire watching voluntarily, they objected to being compelled so the refusal was two-fold: refusing war work and infringement of civil liberties.

COs who were brought back to tribunals because they had failed to comply with their exemption conditions could argue 'reasonable excuse' for non-compliance but if tribunals did not accept this excuse, and they rarely did, the matter was referred back to the Ministry of Labour and National Service. To start with, COs who did not comply with conditions were usually fined – these varied considerably from £5 through to a maximum of £100. If the objector did not pay the fine, a prison sentence might be imposed that could be anything up to a maximum of 15 months. There was no right of return to an appeal tribunal. Usually once an objector had served a prison term, he or she was left alone.

Sidney Greaves was a Quaker and registered as a conscientious objector. He was working in local government and his tribunal, which was in Birmingham, gave him exemption provided he remained in his job. He refused to comply, resigned from his job, and in due course appeared in Bow Street, London, where he was sentenced to six months hard labour in Wormwood Scrubs. Conditions were 'appalling' and 'insanitary'. He was locked in his cell in the early evening, usually at about five-thirty and not let out again until around seven the next morning. Having only the usual bucket in his cell, made slopping out in the morning a disgusting experience. Greaves was assigned to sewing buttonholes for uniforms, until he found out that the uniforms were for the Royal Navy, at which point he objected and was switched to making prison socks. He found prison warders were very hostile to COs: 'They made it very clear we were regarded as scum' and considered that people who were in for violence and robbery were better treated. Following his release from prison, Greaves joined other conscientious objectors, working with the homeless at the Hungerford Club under Charing Cross Station.

A square peg in a round hole
Another objector who refused to comply with a tribunal's decision was Stan Iveson. Born in Lancashire in 1912, he began working as a weaver in the local mill when he left school. After a while Stan went into the building trade, eventually becoming a plumber. A socialist, he was closely involved with the Socialist Sunday School as a child, and later became very active with the Independent Labour Party (ILP), helping to organise strikes, going on demonstrations and running soup kitchens during the Depression. When war came Stan registered as a

conscientious objector but, as was fairly common with political objectors, his local tribunal dismissed his case and ordered his name to be taken off the CO register. The appellate tribunal upheld the decision and he was subsequently fined for failing to attend a medical examination. Stan continued to refuse and was imprisoned for six months in Walton Prison, Liverpool where, according to an interview he gave to photographer Daniel Meadows in 1976, he was probably 'treated one of the best of anyone in prison' largely because he was the only plumber in the prison.

While serving this sentence, Stan's case was reviewed by an appellate tribunal and this time it was decided to register him as a conscientious objector, conditional on working on the land, in a hospital, or in ambulance or civil defence services. However, he refused on political grounds to take up any of these options and once again appeared in court. Stan's case was described in *The Leader*, a socialist newspaper whose editor was then Fenner Brockway.

In an article headed 'Plumber on Farm Would be Square Peg' (13 August 1943) the newspaper stated: 'For failing to comply with the conditions on which he was registered by the Appellate Tribunal as a conscientious objector, Stanley Iveson (31) ... appeared before the local magistrates on Saturday. Mr A.B. Roebuck, prosecuting on behalf of the Ministry of Labour and National Service ... reminded the Bench that for an offence of this kind a person was liable to a penalty of twelve months' imprisonment, or £50, or both. Iveson, a plumber by occupation ... had absolutely defied the authorities, saying he was going to do the work he selected for himself, and when in the course of an interview, he was asked if he intended to take up agricultural work which had been offered to him at Ulverston, he replied "No, that is not the work I promised to do" ... Addressing the Bench, the defendant said he welcomed this opportunity of stating why he should not be in those surroundings that morning ... he was in no way ashamed of standing there and facing this charge, but he wished to explain why he had not taken up the land work ... He was a trained building trades craftsmen ... and he had not yet found a plumber who would be happy milking a cow or digging a ditch ... "When this war started we were told there would be no square pegs in round holes this time, but I submit that a plumber on a farm is definitely a square peg in a round hole.

"I am employed on what I consider to be an A1 priority job – doing plumbing work in working class homes. I would like to thank the

Labour Exchange officials for attempting to get me a job; I only wish their efforts had been as great when I was signing on in 1933. We were told when the war began that wealth would be conscripted, but wealth and property are the only two things that are still left untouched. I have only one thing to offer – my labour – and I propose to offer that in the best market open to me. If Herbert Morrison [Labour politician and then Home Secretary who had been a conscientious objector in the First World War] has a conscience, it must be troubling him now for sending me to gaol for doing what he did in the last war." ... The magistrates then retired to consider the case in private, on their return the Mayor ... reminded Iveson that they were not concerned with his conscientious objections ... what they had to consider was the fact that he had failed to comply with the condition.'

The magistrates imposed a fine of £25, or three months imprisonment. After Iveson told them that he did not even have 25 shillings and would not pay the fine anyway, he was sentenced to three months imprisonment.

Composer Michael Tippett might also have been seen as a square peg in a round hole. A humanitarian and pacifist, he registered as a conscientious objector and was given exemption conditional on doing full-time ARP service, land work or fire service. Yet, as he was then director of music at Morley College in South London, Michael refused to comply with the conditions because he argued that music was his greatest contribution to society. As a result, and despite a plea from composer Vaughan Williams, he was imprisoned in Wormwood Scrubs for three months, just one of many musicians and artists and indeed others whose talents could have been put to so much better use. While in prison, Tippet sewed mailbags and helped with a small prison orchestra. Perhaps ironically, his great anti-war opera *King Priam* was performed in May 1962 as part of the events marking the opening of the new Coventry Cathedral, destroyed during the Blitz in November 1940. The following night Benjamin Britten's *War Requiem*, specially commissioned for the event, was performed. Britten too was a pacifist and conscientious objector, originally directed into the NCC but subsequently given unconditional exemption. In 1958 Tippett was elected honorary president of the PPU, a post that he held until his death in 1998.

'People come to pacifism for many reasons. My own conviction is based on the incompatibility of the arts of modern war with the concept I hold of what a man is at all. That good men do these acts I am well aware. But I hold their actions to spring from an inability or unwillingness to face the fact that modern wars are debasing all our moral coinage to a greater degree than we are gaining anything politically valuable.' Michael Tippett, *Abundance of Creation*, (1975 edition).

Assertive women

In January 1942 Constance ('Connie') Bolam became the very first woman in Britain to be sent to prison as a conscientious objector. As already described, from 1941 British women of eligible age were being conscripted, either for the women's auxiliary services, or into civilian work but, unless they refused to take up the work, did not necessarily have to appear before tribunals.

A staunch absolutist, Connie Bolam had appeared before a tribunal in front of the somewhat notorious Judge Richardson, who had told her that while the panel members had common sense, she had none. A parlour maid, who was working for Kitty Alexander, also a conscientious objector, Connie was registered conditionally on doing land, canteen, or hospital work, all of which she refused to do. Appearing in Newcastle Magistrates' Court on 7 January 1942, she told the court that she disagreed with war in all its shapes and forms and would not take up any work she was told to do. She said it was only because of the war that she was being told to work in a hospital – it would not have happened in peacetime. She was fined 40 shillings, which she refused to pay and sent to Durham Prison for a month, where she worked in the prison laundry. Prisoners were often given jobs to do in their cells and she was told to knit socks for soldiers – not surprisingly, she refused. Fearing publicity, the prison authorities released her a few days early.

Judge Richardson believed that young women COs were more assertive than young men. Either way, many women, on grounds of conscience, followed Connie Bolam into prison. One was her employer Kitty Alexander. Another was Stella St John, who had trained as a vet before the war and was active in the Fellowship of Reconciliation

(FoR), organising their membership files. Before the war, Stella had been active in the peace movement, attending meetings and going on marches. When war came she continued working for FoR and the PPU and held some veterinary clinics. Believing it was not possible to opt out completely, Stella also did 48 hours a month voluntary ambulance and first aid service: 'in the Blitz areas, in Marylebone, right in the middle of it, we had a lot of quiet nights when nothing happened, other nights when it did. Working with the upper classes, New Cavendish Street, Harley Street ... they respected my pacifist views, they were very nice about it, they weren't particularly patriotic minded there.' She was also involved with the Hungerford Shelter, and so was fully engaged in socially useful work.

By 1942, however, new legislation, namely the Civil Defence (Employment & Offences) Order, made work with the ambulance service compulsory. Stella St John formally refused to continue with her ambulance work, explaining her position in a letter that she wrote to the authorities on 4 February 1942: 'In view of the fact that part-time work for the London Auxiliary Ambulance Service becomes compulsory under the new Order, I should like to make it clear that I am only willing to continue under the same conditions as present, or in an emergency would give as much time as I had available. In my case I am not prepared to accept the principle of compulsion for war purposes, but must retain the right at all times to act according to my conscience as a Christian Pacifist. I must therefore feel free to accept at any time work which I might consider to be of more benefit to the community.' In subsequent statements, Stella expanded on this, saying that in her opinion the work she was already doing was 'of real and lasting value to the community'.

The authorities did not accept her argument and she was called before a Women's Panel, which channelled women into war service: 'There were three women ... and they directed me the first time to make records in the War Office, whatever that meant but I said I wouldn't do it and they summoned you and it became an ordinary court case ... a magistrate's court ... the first time the magistrate gave me a week to change my mind so I just had to wait a week and then do it all over again. They said they couldn't understand, men were fighting and weren't you willing to do anything ... to help them. I didn't want to do anything connected with the war, I thought I was doing all I could in the community and he just said "Oh, it's a blank refusal, six weeks" ... I don't think he could do anything else.'

Stella St John was sent to Holloway Prison in 1943 for refusing to be directed into war work. She was taken down immediately: 'Donald Soper was allowed to come and say goodbye to me and then we went in the Black Maria, with the other prisoners and they stopped at Rochester Row police station, picked up more and we went to Holloway … they weren't conscientious objectors, just ordinary people, a bit of everything, I had no contact in the van.'

Stella knew men who had gone to Wormwood Scrubs but she did not know any women COs who had gone to prison, and so was not sure what to expect. In the event: 'It was as bad as I expected, it wasn't any better … but you do get used to it. I thought by the end of the month that awful as it was, it was bearable.'

Stella St John served a month in Holloway, with two weeks remission for good behaviour. Her case was reported in the *Evening Standard* and other newspapers and she later wrote a booklet about her experiences, *A Prisoner's Log*, which was published as a pamphlet by the Howard League for Prison Reform in 1944. There is a copy with her papers in the document section of the Imperial War Museum. In the pamphlet she describes the process of registration, when she was locked into 'little metal boxes with wire on top … given two slices of bread and marge and a pint of cocoa … my first experience of prison cocoa and although very hungry, I couldn't cope with it especially as it was very tepid.' On her first day, she was visited by the prison chaplain: 'We did not get on too well as he is not fond of conscientious objectors. However he offered a prayer that while I had time to think it over I might be guided alright.'

For the first fortnight Stella worked in the prison laundry 'notoriously a place people dislike. The first few days were extremely unpleasant. Several of us who were new had no idea what to do, when asked we were told, "Don't ask me I'm too busy" … We then just stood doing nothing and got cursed for that!' She was moved onto cleaning, which 'consisted of getting a bucket of cold water (not hot), getting on our knees and washing the stone and wooden floors with people walking over them all the time … We were not allowed to wear kneelers so our knees were in real agony … we were very cold.'

From there Stella was moved onto 'mangling, hanging clothes up – got you a bit warm … You stand there and scrub clothes all day long, it isn't bad really. You are at least free from abuse.' Finally Stella was put in the workroom, where there were two other COs. This was 'a great joy because we could by gradual wrangling get next to each other. Able to talk. Worked on pants for men prisoners the whole time because we could not do war work ... the prisoner who gave out work was sympathetic and kept us supplied with them.' Other prisoners were making kit bags for the army. It was monotonous work, six hours daily, on hard seats 'but as we were together and could talk we had much to be thankful for'.

There were air raids as well. 'The first one was my first night in prison. I had just got into bed when the siren went: immediately every light in the building was extinguished ... because most of the roof is glass ... As soon as the guns began, officers started to unlock the cell doors. This naturally took a bit of time and those who were not unlocked started frantically ringing their bells, shouting and banging on the walls and doors. The result was to create a feeling of panic.'

Stella did not experience much criticism for being a conscientious objector, though some prisoners were perplexed: 'The prisoners are usually amazed when you say you are in for conscientious objection to war. On the whole they are very tolerant ... some even being sympathetic, saying "Good luck to you. I don't hold with this war, but I wouldn't get put in here for it." Others merely look at you as if you were mad. I only came across three women ... who were really antagonistic ... The chaplain was the most antagonistic. He had no use for the pacifist position and thought it anti-Christian.' Donald Soper was there to meet Stella when she left Holloway; the chaplain was present too and on hearing that Stella had not changed her mind, said he would pray for her. After leaving prison, she continued working at the Hungerford Club.

Interestingly as Stella St John was leaving prison, another woman CO was going in. She was the crystallographer Kathleen Lonsdale, a Quaker and pacifist, who served a month in Holloway also for refusing to be directed into compulsory fire watching duties. As a mother with three children under the age of 14, she could have gained exemption but chose to take her stand against war and against what she saw as the denial of civil liberties caused by compulsion.

Kathleen Wigham was also sent to prison for refusing to take up civilian work as directed. Having trained as a special needs teacher for young children, when war began she was working in a health food shop in Blackburn. She registered as a conscientious objector and in 1942 was directed to do hospital work. She appeared before an industrial tribunal and explained that she would not comply 'because I object to doing any work which will relieve anyone else to do military service'. After a few months, she received a summons for £5 and was given ten days to pay. She did nothing and after ten days was summonsed to appear at court in Blackburn:

'I went and stated my views against war and the reason why I had refused to be conscripted into industrial work. And they actually did their best to persuade me to pay the fine; they said, "We don't want to send people like you to prison, can you pay your fine?" So I said, "I can pay it but I'm not prepared to." "Well, would you pay it if we said five shillings a week?" I said, "No, it isn't a question of hardship. I've had half a dozen people wanting to pay the fine for me but I just refuse to take their offers. I have … a conscientious objection to doing this sort of work."'

The court even contacted Kathleen's employer to find out if he would pay the fine, which with one son a CO in prison and another being directed into war work he was prepared to do, but Kathleen told him not to. On 2 July 1942 she appeared in court again and once more the magistrate tried to persuade her to pay her fine; however, when he realised she was determined, he sentenced her to the shortest term he could – 14 days in Strangeways, Manchester. Kathleen was taken down to the cells, allowed a brief visit with her mother and a Quaker friend, then taken to Strangeways in a police car, her escorts still trying to persuade her to pay the fine, saying, 'Prison's not for a girl like you, you're too sensitive.'

In 1980 Kathleen Wigham was interviewed by the Imperial War Museum. She gave a long and very detailed account of her time in prison, which is fascinating to listen to and very personal. It clearly was an extremely stressful experience. She describes how, when she entered the prison, she felt as if she was completely 'cut off from the outside world … you're handed over, the police car and the police lady and what you might term your kind friends are all gone. And you enter in there and the voices immediately are harsh, and shouting; there's no one soft spoken, or so it seemed.' Having given her personal details: 'I'd been told … at the reception desk … I must tell them that I was a vegetarian and then I could get the vegetarian meals … I said to the lady "Would you mind putting down that I'm a vegetarian?" And she just said, "You'll be treated like the other ones here, you haven't come to a convalescent home." And after that I didn't dare say anything else.'

No vegetarian meals were forthcoming, so Kathleen only ate porridge and potatoes, which were 'not only cooked in their jackets – which I appreciated – but with soil and tails and eyes all in as well; you had to pick and choose what you could eat, and you could hardly cut it out because the knife is so blunt.' She left any meat on her dish, which eventually led to a very unpleasant visit from the prison doctor. She explained that she was vegetarian, the doctor looked into her eyes and, turning to the warder, said: "You can find her a bed in the hospital, she's barmy." ... And I was very close to tears because I felt his visit had been unnecessary ... and his remark was extremely rude.'

A wardress came in, told her to collect her blankets and then verbally abused her: 'She said to me: "Our men are out fighting for sluts like you ... If I had my way you'd certainly be hanging from the end of a rope" ... And prodding me all the time ... giving me not just a prod, a nudge almost knocking me over ... I just said nothing, I just found it difficult to talk. A lump was in my throat and I was very close to tears ... then she took me to the hospital part ... to a ward and said to a sister "She's had to come over from the prison side and she's one of those bloody conchies." And I can remember the matron just sort of tapping me on the shoulder and pushing me on.'

Kathleen was shocked by the state of some of the women in the hospital wing but the matron turned out to be kindly, 'the first person since leaving the police officers that had spoken in what I call a soft tone; so it was like music to my ears'. The matron put her to sewing, mending nurses' aprons, and took her around as a helper in the prison maternity ward, pushing the trolley.

In Kathleen's second week she was allowed a Quaker visitor, George Sutherland, the principle of Durham Hall; her friends had heard she had been moved to the hospital and wanted news. Sutherland and the Manchester Quakers also obtained permission for Kathleen to attend a Quaker meeting in the male side of the prison. This was very unusual and for Kathleen it was an enormous pleasure, hampered slightly by the fact that the prison wardress who accompanied her insisted that Kathleen wore woollen stockings with nothing to hold them up.

In Kathleen's opinion, the wardress was rather nervous. She 'pushed herself in front of me and was going to walk right past in her official way. But Edgar Upperton [a Quaker prison visitor] stopped her and said "Just a minute, Friend, we shake hands, we welcome each other. You're very welcome to this meeting; you can forget your prison uniform, you're one of us." ... she was so surprised, she just managed to smile.' As the male prisoners came in, they shook hands as is the Quaker way; among them was one of Kathleen's friends, Stan Iveson 'who gave me a wink'. The meeting was very important to Kathleen: 'It was just a comfort to me ... when I had been feeling down and wondering whether I had done the right thing; it gave me hope and the spirit to go on.'

Kathleen spent eight days in the hospital wing and six days in the prison. Like many others, she found her cells claustrophobic and bare; the slopping out process was disgusting and the harshness of the environment overwhelming. Air raids were also alarming: 'hearing the bombs and knowing you were a prisoner and couldn't get out.' Of her mental state while in prison she said: 'Were my nerves affected by it? I'm quite sure they were. I believe I must have been fairly highly-strung and very, very close to tears. I cried an awful lot – on my own ... I came to ask myself whether I shouldn't pay my fine and then realised that I couldn't; there was something stopping me ... And I was very grateful that it was only going to be two weeks, because I felt sure I wouldn't have lasted any longer ... without going mental myself.'

Chapter 10

Discrimination and Abuse

'People were hostile to COs ... people didn't understand how brave they were.'

Joan Pasco

In his interview with the Imperial Museum, Tony Parker commented that 'it was remarkably tolerant to introduce legislation for conscription and simultaneously the 'conscience clause.' Several objectors acknowledged the consideration they experienced and many, among them veteran COs of the First World War, commented on how much more tolerant the climate was for conscientious objectors this time around. Whether this was because of Britain's reputation for fair play and acceptance of those seen as slightly oddball; whether, as Denis Hayes considered, it was deliberate official policy; or whether conscientious objectors were simply more familiar than in the previous war, is difficult to say. However, despite the greater tolerance, conscientious objectors as a whole and as individuals experienced a considerable amount of antagonism, prejudice, discrimination and sometimes downright vitriolic hatred from members of the public, the press and employers. Not surprisingly attitudes to COs were particularly bad during 1940 and 1941 when the war situation looked bleak and all British resources, civilian and military, were focused on total war.

Public attitudes
Social research organisation Mass Observation carried out a number of surveys into public attitudes towards pacifists and conscientious objectors between April and June 1940 and found that most people they interviewed were fairly ambivalent, although antagonism

noticeably increased in May 1940 when German troops overran Norway and Holland. Attitudes varied from a small percentage (seven to nine) who approved of conscientious objectors, and might themselves have felt they would have liked to have taken that stand, through to others (about 40 per cent) who were fairly antagonist and believed firm measures should be taken against them, including shutting them away for the duration. One or two even thought COs should be shot like traitors. Between the two extremes most people surveyed did not approve of COs but felt they had the right to hold the views they did, perhaps demonstrating that most British people supported freedom of speech. Even so conscientious objectors who were featured in the press or who held public office often came under considerable attack.

Leonard Frank Bunnewell was a Yarmouth town councillor and a member of the Independent Labour Party (ILP). A pacifist, in 1941 he registered as a conscientious objector and was granted exemption, conditional on getting a job in food production or distribution. His case was reported in the local press and led to a flurry of very angry letters. One, signed anonymously 'More Proud Than Ever to be a Tory' stormed:

'With disgust I read in last week's *Mercury* that Councillor L.F. Bunnewell is a C.O. This, I hope is an exception rather than the rule for Labour. No doubt Mr Bunnewell was crying "Help Abyssinia" and "Send arms to Spain" during their respective crises. Might I ask if he holds a ration book? If so it is from our brave merchantmen that he is taking food. Does he possess a gas mask? Surely Hitler won't bother to gas him!'

Another letter, signed 'Yarmouthian' stated that 'many people would like to know how he "got away with it"', and expressed surprise that 'he did not seem to appeal on religious grounds, which I thought were the only grounds under which an applicant could successfully appeal'. The writer hoped that 'the voters in the ward he represents on the Town Council will see to it at the first opportunity that Councillor Bunnewell will no longer be anything but plain Mr Bunnewell. I am sure that voters in my home town have no desire – to whatever party they belong – to be represented in the Council by a C.O. 'Other letters too, one signed by 'A Mother' and another by 'Old Yarmouthian', also a woman, expressed their disgust at Bunnewell being a conscientious objector, and hoped that the voters would 'wake up' and vote him off the Council, particularly those who 'have husbands and sons serving in the fighting forces'.

In their surveys Mass Observation found that the most critical members of the public tended to be women and older men; younger men were often more accepting of COs. Bunnewell did receive a few letters in his defence, including one from an F. Bolton, who argued that 'a man is entitled to his opinions' stating that 'Bunnewell ... has a perfect right to stand for what he believes is right ... If there is a new world to come out of this war ... it will be made by a new generation who have vision and faith in the future, and who are prepared to march forward into the light and sunshine of to-morrow.'

The correspondence was closed but re-emerged in 1945, after the war, when Bunnewell, who must have been a good councillor, was elected Alderman. Once again there were many letters to the press, some protesting, others supportive. One protest came from a woman whose only son, Jim Edis, 'a dearly-loved lad' had died 'in Japanese hands after being a prisoner of war for two years, one of the gallant R.A.F. band'. It was perhaps not surprising that she found it 'preposterous and ironic that in a town like Yarmouth, with so many of her sons in the Royal Norfolks, who have suffered loss of liberty, been tortured, maimed, and died, should be represented on the aldermanic bench by a conscientious objector'.

Rather bravely Bunnewell replied through the letters' page, expressing his sympathy and understanding. He had obviously known Jim Edis because he described him as 'an outstanding young man; his idealism made him so ... his deep interest in religion and philosophy, science and economics made his death not only a loss to his relatives but to the community'. He went on: 'But it is just there that the force of the pacifist's arguments comes in, for, surely there must be something intrinsically evil in war if it destroys, as it does, so many of the "loveliest and the best". Jim Edis came into this world, I believe, to live, to have dreams of a world made better, and to help that world come into being. He was destroyed by war.' He finished by hoping that maybe he 'as a pacifist, can serve some useful purpose in our local government which needs to do such a great deal of constructive work'.

Not surprisingly Edis's mother was extremely angry and wrote in saying so; other letter writers supported her. Others though wrote in defence of Bunnewell, including another bereaved mother who hoped that, 'If by being a conscientious objector he and others like him can in the slightest way help to put a stop to our boys being sent to certain death, I and thousands of mothers are for him every time'. There was also a letter from a writer who signed himself 'Air Mechanic' and stated that he felt 'it is time that someone should take up arms in support of the true conscientious objector, for surely a person who is prepared to stand before the whole world and state that he will not fight because he believes in his religion, has more guts than many a man who is now in the fighting Services'. All in all it was an interesting post bag, reflective of the different public attitudes towards conscientious objectors.

Many conscientious objectors whose names appeared in the press received hate mail, among them Reginald Porcas, who had refused to register as a CO in 1939 as a matter of principle. He received a number of very nasty and abusive letters, most of which were anonymous, calling him among other names: 'skunk', 'white livered cur', 'scum' and telling him that 'if this country is not worth fighting for − go and live in Germany'. Not every conscientious objector received such abusive letters but for those that did they added to a feeling of being persecuted and isolated, which many objectors experienced. Porcas, who had been a civil servant, worked with the CBCO as an observer and after the war joined the Associated Press as a reporter.

'Perverts' and 'Fifth Columnists'

The attitude of the press, like that of the public, varied considerably but was often at its most hysterical during times of emergency or when the war was going badly for Britain. Then as now it was usually the popular press that could be most vitriolic, accusing conscientious objectors of being traitors, cowards and perverts. During the British retreat from Dunkirk, in a black-edged editorial headed 'Pacifism' and dated 2 June 1940, the *Sunday Pictorial* published a splenetic rant against conscientious objectors, storming that the paper: 'declares war on the nauseating young men who pretend that they believe in "peace". And this weekend, when B.E.F. heroes set foot again on English soil, provides an appropriate moment to strike the first blow.'

The writer described pacifists as 'elegant sissies who fester the restaurants of London, gossiping like girls about their "hearts" and "inner souls" … weedy, long-haired intellectuals who enjoyed the honey in the peace days and now go pale at the thought of defending the land from which it flowed' and 'cynics of the parasitical professions'. The paper then finished its appallingly vitriolic and, to our eyes, politically incorrect editorial, by insisting in emphatic capitals that: 'THESE YOUNG PERVERTS, IDIOTS AND RACKETEERS ARE DANGEROUS … PUT THE BUNCH OF THEM BEHIND BARBED WIRE.'

Not all newspapers plumbed such vitriolic depths as the *Sunday Pictorial*, but several either criticised or poked fun at conscientious objectors, many of them focusing on unfortunate responses given by COs at their tribunals, taking a mocking tone and highlighting any odd behaviour, no doubt in an attempt to stir up anti-CO attitudes among their readership. The *Daily Mail* consistently took a strong anti-conscientious objector line, calling them 'shirkers', objecting to the money paid to COs in civilian employment, and generally taking whatever opportunity the paper could find to criticise them. The *Sunday Graphic* too complained bitterly that 'conchies' were being paid too much, which helped to reinforce any ill-informed prejudice.

Some newspapers did their best to ensure a balanced coverage. The *Daily Herald* was one of various newspapers that consistently drew attention to prejudiced comments from tribunal chairmen. On 3 March 1940 the paper covered a London tribunal where the chairman, Alderman Marshall, responding to a conscientious objector who said he would welcome the Germans because he trusted them 'as his fellow men', stated: 'It is quite obvious from your last answer that you have not got any conscience.' In its editorial comment the paper stated that: 'The *Daily Herald* completely disagrees with the young man's attitude. But it claims that he is entitled to hold that attitude. For Alderman Marshall's wisecrack it can find no justification whatsoever. Such superficial comments are a poor advertisement for the impartiality of the tribunals.'

Leftish-liberal newspapers such as the *News Chronicle* and socialist papers such as the *New Leader* took a far more sympathetic line, with editorials defending COs and frequently highlighting injustices at tribunals. Quite a number drew attention to Judge Richardson's ill-judged comments and the *Daily Chronicle* took a leading role in highlighting the plight of Stanley Hilton, the Jehovah's Witness who fell foul of the 'cat and mouse' practice. Naturally pacifist newspapers such as *Peace News* supported COs and headlined any injustices, but their readership of course was by definition a sympathetic one.

Pacifists and conscientious objectors were frequently accused of being cowards, Fifth Columnists, Nazi sympathisers or Nazi enablers.

On 15 April 1939 the *Hastings & St Leonards Observer* printed what one pacifist reader described as 'more than a column of vituperation' from an anonymous scribe 'Britain for the British', who launched a ferocious attack on the 'anti-recruiting clerics' of the Peace Pledge Union. The writer claimed that the PPU's effect was such that: 'Scared into emotional refusal to fight by war-funk propaganda, wretched lads who are cowards are encouraged to make hypocrites of themselves ... by pretending religious objection to war, and then praised as heroes because they are not afraid to break their country's laws and go to prison, in order to escape danger or death in battle.' In the writer's view: 'The nation is to be stampeded into surrender by peace riots', and he invited the Chief Constable of Hastings to consider whether there was not '*prima facie* evidence that the propaganda of the P.P.U. is seditious interference with ... recruiting'. Not surprisingly local peace activists and organisers of the Hastings PPU, Mary and Kenneth Wray, together with other pacifists rapidly put pen to paper and flooded the letters column in protest the following week.

In April 1940 the *Evening Standard* accused 'cranks, pacifists and paid agents' of being engaged 'in subversive propaganda to undermine the nation's war effort' and made the extraordinary claim that 'it is believed that both Berlin and Moscow are contributing funds for the peace-at-any-price campaigns in Britain', before going on to state that 'Members of the anti-war organisations in Britain ... are serving Hitler's cause by opposing war'. Such attitudes were not uncommon and continued until well after the war. As late as 16 June 1954 *The Times* published a letter from Lindsay Dewar, Bishops' College, Hertfordshire, in which he stated: 'Pacifists should be reminded that their teaching is liable to have the very opposite effect to that which they desire; it may precipitate war. There is definite evidence that this is what happened in 1939 when the activities of the Peace Pledge Union influenced Hitler in thinking that in no circumstances would this country intervene in a European war.'

In fact there never was any shred of evidence whatsoever to back up this claim. This however did not stop Dr Chavasse, Bishop of Rochester, in July 1958, never one to let a few facts get in the way of a rousing sermon, on being asked who was responsible for the stupidity and iniquity of the Second World War, from replying: 'Whose hands are red with the blood of the tortured victims of the Gestapo and bombed civilians ... It was the pacifists of the Peace Pledge Union who successfully tied the hands of the Government ... and turned the League of Nations into a figure of fun', (*The Times* 14 July 1958).

During the inter-war years, pacifist groups had experienced very little hostility, possibly reflecting the anti-war attitudes of the general population, even if most people chose not to become involved. With the outbreak of war attitudes hardened and a number of individuals and groups, particularly the PPU, came under surveillance. On 23 February 1940 *The Times* reported a debate in the House of Commons concerning the 'subversive activities' of the PPU, with particular reference to the charge that they were picketing employment exchanges. This charge, as already mentioned, was quite incorrect but in his reply Sir John Anderson MP, who gave his name to the Anderson shelter, stated that 'The activities of this organisation are being carefully watched'. By March 1940 PPU members were being arrested for distributing leaflets and newspapers, including *Peace News*, and police were frequently seen at PPU meetings, taking notes. In May 1940 six PPU officers – Alex Wood, Morris Rowntree, Stuart Morris, John Barclay, Ronald Henry Smith and Sydney Todd – were arrested and appeared in court charged with 'an endeavour to cause among persons in HM Service disaffection likely to lead to breaches of their duty'. The cause was a PPU poster, which carried the slogan: 'War will cease when men refuse to fight. What are YOU going to do about it?' The men argued that the poster was not directed at the armed forces but at members of the public. They were found guilty although the Attorney General considering them to be 'honourable men' merely bound them over to keep the peace. The PPU withdrew the poster.

Sacked for being a CO

Muriel McMillan (neé Smith) was one of the fortunate conscientious objectors: her firm kept her on during the war. Muriel worked with an insurance company and when she registered as a CO was perhaps surprised to find that her boss was very tolerant: 'the whole firm was very tolerant ... we had one or two men who were also COs and there were very few who were not extremely tolerant to us ... I worked with two other [women], one was completely tolerant, the other ... I know she didn't think much of us but there was really no unpleasantness between us.' However, one of her brothers, Arthur, who worked as a dental surgeon for the local authority, was sacked because he was a conscientious objector.

Arthur Smith's situation was not unusual. Many COs were discriminated against: they were either sacked from their jobs or, as already mentioned, had great difficulty in finding work. Reginald Bottini had been working as a shipping clerk for some years with a firm in London and when the time came he went to the company secretary, Mr Brown, and told him he was going to register as a conscientious objector: 'it reminded me of the advertisement of the man in the chemist's shop who wondered whether Howell's aspirin was the best. He went *white*, poor man. He'd never had such a shock … because I was such a good clerk and generally reliable.' Mr Brown said Bottini would have to see the deputy chairman, Mr Stewart, which he did: 'Mr Stewart used some insulting expressions and said, "Get rid of him!" No one dared to speak to me during that week. Being thoroughly awkward, I enjoyed making everyone feel embarrassed … and marched out very proudly.'

Eric Farley too was sacked for being a CO. In December 1940 he received a letter from his employers, Battersea Borough Council, telling him that following a meeting of the Council he had been given a month's notice. It was legal to be a conscientious objector but there was no law that said an employer could not dismiss a member of staff who was a CO, even if tribunals had given an objector exemption, conditional on remaining in his or her existing job. In the spring and summer of 1940 public dislike and distrust of conscientious objectors reached an all-time high and there was considerable resentment of, and hostility towards, COs who were employed both in the public and private sectors.

In February 1940 the *Daily Herald* reported that women in the Norwich district were walking miles to pay their rents rather than pay them to the rent-collector, who was a conscientious objector. The employee, John Kenneth Dalton, was dismissed on a month's notice. Local fire brigades too were refusing to work with COs or actively discriminating against them. On 23 June 1940 the *Evening Standard* quoted the chief of Skipton Fire Brigade, who had told his committee that he was not prepared to help 'conchies' until after everyone else: 'Conchies, I suppose, have a right to their own opinions and views, but I think it right that those people who are prepared to defend their freedom should have the first call on the services of men who give up their time and leisure to protect lives and property.' As already described, farmers were not prepared to work with COs nor were many private companies prepared to keep COs on their staff.

'I would sooner put a handle on the organ than have a Conscientious Objector on the staff of my church.' Rev. J. Byrnell, vicar St James's Church, Selby, (*Yorkshire Evening News*, 10 May 1940).

Local authority employees, whether council workers or teachers, were particularly vulnerable, with many people resenting them being paid out of the public purse. Given the prevailing climate, councils up and down the country debated the issue and during spring and summer 1940 one town, district or rural council after another voted to dismiss COs from their employ. Often the decision was by an overwhelming majority. On 25 June 1940 the *Daily Dispatch* reported that Stockport Town Council had decided by 47 votes to two to dismiss its conscientious objector employees as well as others 'who have engaged in propaganda calculated to influence people against military or civil defence services or the successful prosecution of the war'. Local and national newspapers reported that Chatham Town Council had decided to discharge a CO on their staff; West Bromwich had voted to dismiss COs from their employ, so too had Devon County Council and Nottingham. Plymouth Education Committee followed suit in June 1940, making an exception only for COs who had told their tribunals they were willing to undertake non-combatant duties. By July 1940, according to the CBCO's records, as many as 86 local authorities had decided to dismiss COs; 33 to suspend them for the duration of the war; and 13 councils had voted to put conscientious objectors onto soldiers' pay. Only 16 councils chose to keep COs on their staff.

Reports of council debates around the issue of COs show that quite a number of councillors and council officers, caught up in the wartime atmosphere, were just as prejudiced as other members of the public. These contain comments that COs were shirkers, cowards and 'curs', who were only fortunate not to be in Nazi Germany. Actually many conscientious objectors were acutely aware of the freedom of expression that they enjoyed in Britain as opposed to the repression they would experience in Germany. Others seriously wrestled with the problem before coming down on the side of deciding that those who chose not to take up military service had lost their right to be employed by public bodies.

Some councillors though were seriously concerned not only that they were operating against government policy but also showing themselves to be just as authoritarian as Nazi Germany. In November 1940 a local paper reported that Councillor Romanes of Essex County Council had moved the resolution to keep COs on staff, because 'if they refused to employ [a man] ... because he held views which were not popular ... they were going exactly the same way that Germany went in the case of racial troubles. If a man had a conscience he could no more go against his conscience than a Jew could help being a Jew.' The government too was not altogether happy with decisions that councils were making. On 1 August 1940, Ernest Bevin replying to a question in the House of Commons about COs' pay being brought in line with men serving in the armed forces, said: 'I am getting on with it as fast as I can; but I am not being assisted in this difficult and technical job by the action of a number of local authorities in taking the law into their own hands.' He was referring to York City Council, which among others, had just decided to discriminate against COs.

Other government ministers too were unhappy about the decisions that councils were making and there were protests about the situation from many eminent individuals. On 16 August 1940 the Archbishop of York wrote to *The Times* deploring the fact that public bodies were dismissing conscientious objectors and saying: 'I regard this as utterly deplorable and in the deepest sense unpatriotic. We are fighting for freedom, including freedom of conscience as its most vital and sensitive element. The State has recognised the reality of conscientious objection to military service, and it is part of our glory that it does this.' The Archbishop said it would be perfectly reasonable to put a CO onto the same financial position as a man in the forces 'but to deprive him of employment is to frustrate the action of the State and destroy our most effective witness to our own cause ... I hope Christian public opinion ... will set itself against this essentially Nazi policy'. In the end however, little could be done about the situation and for those COs who were dismissed, the situation added to the difficulties, financial and emotional, that many experienced as a result of discrimination.

Risk to young minds

Discrimination against COs existed in the public and the private sectors and there were some surprising decisions. In 1940 the Co-operative Society, known then as now for its ethical trading, made the extraordinary decision to dismiss conscientious objectors from its staff.

On 10 July 1940 an Anti-Conscientious Objector League in Blackpool sent out letters to businesses who had COs on their staff warning them of this fact and staff in a number of firms threatened to strike if COs were not dismissed. On 10 July 1940 *The Times* reported that the Association of Ex-Service Civil Servants had issued a statement protesting against the employment of COs in the service, urging that employers should take an oath of loyalty and there should be a campaign to rid the service of 'undesirable elements'.

One issue that caused considerable debate was whether conscientious objectors, who were working as teachers, should be allowed to remain in their post. The biggest anxiety was clearly that they might corrupt the thinking of the young. On 11 April 1940 *The Times* reported a question from the MP for Tiverton who asked the President of the Board of Education, Herweld Ramsbotham, whether he was aware that a 'considerable number of conscientious objectors were being granted exemption on condition that they remained in the teaching profession and whether, in view of the danger to the country of the spread of the views of these people, he would take steps to ensure that they were not employed in any schools which received State grants'. Ramsbotham replied that this was up to local education authorities but he had no reason to suppose that the people concerned would not uphold the principles of teaching and that 'political propaganda' would not be introduced into schools. Not everybody felt the same and in July 1940 various sections of the press highlighted the situation of two assistant teachers, R.H. Foxley and N.A. Bird, who had been dismissed from Homelands Central School, Torquay because they were members of the PPU. Foxley in fact did not register as a conscientious objector until June 1941.

The debate within the local council, which a month previously had voted to dismiss COs from their staff, was opened by Councillor Naracott, who launched a particularly nasty attack, saying: 'There has been a lot of talk about teachers in schools. I don't understand the meaning of the term Fifth Column, or of the Peace Pledge Union, but I do understand the meaning of the word "traitor" … I think it is really time that something was done. They won't fight, they preach the Fifth Column, they preach the Peace Pledge Union and they are teaching the children the same. If it gets into the mind of the children, they will be like the children of Germany. It is up to us as a Council to see that this thing is stopped.' The motion to have the men fired was proposed by Councillor Perry who stormed: 'We had a decision about conscientious objectors and I think these merchants are one hundred per cent worse ... I move we have them fired.' It was seconded.

Cllr Samways was not at all happy about the motion, pointing out that the men had already taken an oath of allegiance to King and Country, which by this time had become common practice in schools, and pointed out that the men had removed their PPU badges and that one had resigned from the PPU. He also said, 'We must not introduce Hitlerism into this country'. Despite this voice of reason, the motion was carried and was duly reported in the press, the *Torquay Times* of 5 July 1940, even running an editorial on the subject in which it put forward yet again the extraordinarily prejudiced view that the PPU was disseminating 'propaganda more cunning and crafty than anything that so far emanated from the fertile brain of Dr Goebbels' and that 'men and women subscribing to such tenets would have our country lay down arms ... Treachery of such a kind should be dealt with in the most effective way.'

There was an outcry against the decision. Both men were members of the National Union of Teachers (NUT), which launched a protest against the decision, pointing out that the men had been dismissed without being given a hearing. Teachers wrote asking the council to reconsider their decision on the grounds that it completely negated the principle of freedom for which Britain was fighting, as did head teachers and school captains from Aubrey Park Boys School, where one of the teachers had worked previously. Some of the press were very critical. On 1 August 1940 the *Herald Express* in its editorial stated that neither man had ever given any evidence of disloyalty or subversion and that it was 'the most un-English thing I have ever heard of ... No loyal Britisher could say one word in favour of it.' However, despite representations from teachers and the NUT and although there were another two stormy council debates, the council held firm to its original decision.

Intolerance and tolerance

On a personal level the amount of intolerance or hostility that conscientious objectors encountered varied enormously. William Elliot met only a few instances of hostility and those were from members of the public. Apparently they did not cause him distress and he also thought that the armed forces were more tolerant of COs than members of the public. Some other COs felt the same way, among them Denis Hayes, who thought 'Pacifists on the whole got on very well with the people in the forces; the people in the forces on the whole understood the pacifist's viewpoint far better than the administrators or the people who were full of vigour as to the worthiness of the cause … I think there was a certain kind of kinship between them and the conscientious objectors; they were both caught in the system. They had gone one way and the conscientious objector had gone the other … but they understood very well what the conscientious objector stood for.' Clearly this view could not have been applied to those members of the army who beat up COs at Dingle Vale and Ilfracombe.

Most COs in their writings and interviews mention instances of hostility and intolerance directed towards them, many of which have already been mentioned. For some it was a very painful experience; others, being perhaps by nature awkward individuals were unconcerned. Fred and Zoe Vahey, probably because of their absolutist stand and no doubt also because Fred refused to shrink away into the background, were harassed from time to time on suspicion of being spies or harbouring Germans. According to Fred's daughter, Lorna: 'The Home Guard used to raid him with monotonous regularity every time there was a German airman or airplane down or something. My parents were living either in the caravan [a Romany caravan which is still on the land] or this tiny chalet … which had a double bed and a wood stove and that was about all … they used to come in and my father used to take the piss out of them and said: "Have you looked under the bed" … it was probably because he refused to do Home Guard, fire, ambulance, stretcher bearer … he refused to do any of it.

'He decided he wasn't going to cut his hair until the war ended, whether he stuck to that I don't know, but he used to walk around in shorts and this wild, wild hair and beard and he used to get stopped all the time when he came into town. He used to carry his papers in his hand he got stopped so often. It amused him that they thought a spy would walk about being so noticeable. So, although people were a bit hostile, he didn't care.' Eventually, though the harassment stopped. According to Lorna: 'I think fairly rapidly people realised he was just this sort of oddball and he was quite generous and likeable, so I don't think there was any huge tormenting, just the irritant of being checked on all the time.'

Some COs were less concerned about hostility towards them than they were of the effect on friends and family. Muriel McMillan's boss and workmates accepted her but the same could not be said of some of her neighbours. Muriel's two brothers were also COs: 'There was a certain amount [of hostility] though once again most people were very tolerant but there were a few people who were unpleasant both to us and, unfairly, to our parents who, although they backed us up, did not share our views. One or two people up the road studiously ignored us in passing and I think on one occasion accused my brothers of being cowards ... but on the whole people were very tolerant ... there were a few people who very understandably with sons in the forces found it hard to stomach us.' There and again in Muriel's view hostility was never predictable: 'there were those who had their children in the forces and even some of them were killed but who still remained very kind to us; others who had no children were very intolerant to us.'

One CO concerned about the impact of his stand on his close family was Frederick Morel. He wrote regularly to his wife while in prison and in one of his letters referred to some friends, saying 'I was lying in my cell last night thinking and thinking of your very good comrades ... I don't suppose that either of them will come near you now. They make me feel sick.' He encouraged her to go out and spend time with friends in their local ILP branch, who would be supportive. Eric Turner had been a milkman and registered as a conscientious objector. For him the most difficult part 'was the pain and embarrassment I caused my parents ... They could not understand ... why I wanted to be a conscientious objector. This meant that my relationships with my own family, friends and neighbours were much more difficult than going through the tribunal.'

Concern for family continued even after the war. Eric Farley was anxious his stand should not disadvantage his daughter Susannah: 'When I was a child it wasn't that long after the war – I was born in 1954 – a lot of people that I would have been mixing with as a child had lost relatives. My father used to say, "Don't tell people, it's better for you not to tell people".'

Reginald Bottini said that there was 'nobody coming up, as I understand they did in the First World War, with insults and white feathers or leaflets through the door, or screams from agitated women ... just a bleak incomprehension as to how one could take this view.' However, Kathleen Wigham did experience this sort of thing, though her mother coped with it very well: 'There was some hostility. I got a white feather, the sign of cowardice, sent anonymously through the post. It was in a piece of paper in an envelope; it fell out and Mother just picked it up and put it on the fire and said, "We don't want any of them here".' Another CO, Frank Norman, an absolutist who was served time in Lewes Prison and Wormwood Scrubs said that about 60 per cent of his neighbours were antagonistic. One of them, who had formerly held a senior position in the Indian Army and was then aged about 70, used to sing patriotic songs very loudly whenever he saw Frank.

COs dealt with discrimination and abuse as best they could; where possible gaining help and support from other conscientious objectors or sympathetic friends, but the overall effect was often to make them feel like pariahs, excluded from the wider community.

Allowing though for all the victimisation and discrimination there were many COs who also acknowledged that there was a surprising amount of tolerance given the strains of war. William Elliot was a member of the Labour Party, which had decided to support the war, and realised, much like Labour Party members today who opposed the Iraq War, that he and other pacifist Labour Party members were going to have difficulty staying in the Party and would be in a minority. But wanting to maintain the 'traditional ties between the labour movement and the pacifist cause ... I thought that if we had a fellowship, which we could belong to and meet to discuss difficulties arising from the war this would sustain us.'

As a result he and others set up the Labour Pacifist Fellowship, with Reginald Sorensen as chairman and a number of other Labour MPs as members. When the Fellowship was formed in 1940 they incurred some hostility from Labour Party branches. However, as William discovered: 'one of the strange but very wonderful things is how even in wartime, certainly as far as the second war is concerned, there's such tolerance. Reg Sorenson was able to book a room for us at the House of Commons ... we could all turn up for a meeting in spite of the fact that we were running completely counter to what everybody else was doing in those days. I don't think this could happen in any other country in the world.' Elliot put this tolerance down 'very largely to the men who had taken the stand in the first war ... the wonderful stand, it must have impressed itself upon its opponents ... I'm sure that's what created the more tolerant climate.'

Discrimination and hostility directed towards conscientious objectors was at its most intense during the first half of the war. As time progressed, attitudes softened. COs' humanitarian work with the homeless and bombed out civilians, their medical work and work in hospitals, their involvement in civil defence, fire-fighting, bomb disposal and their service abroad with the Friends Ambulance Unit and parachute units won them respect from both military personnel and civilians who worked with them.

Chapter 11

War Ends

'*The Conscientious Objector is building better than he knows.*'
Fenner Brockway

The Second World War ended in 1945: war with Germany ended on 8 May 1945, and with Japan on 15 August 1945. Under the National Service (Release of Conscientious Objectors) Act 1946, conscientious objectors were released from their tribunal conditions, from non-combatant duties in the army and from prison. Ironically, the process of release mirrored that of demobilisation from the armed services, with COs being released by age groups and length of 'service'. The last wartime COs were released in 1947. The end of war did not mean the end of conscription, which continued, as National Service, until 1960, the final registration date being 10 January 1959. As with wartime conscription, there was a conscience clause: between 1 September 1945 and 10 January 1959 just over 9,000 men registered as conscientious objectors.

After six years of war, conscientious objectors, like members of the armed forces and other civilians, had to re-adjust to the post-war world. Some went back into their previous occupations, while others took up new occupations. Even though hostility against COs had certainly diminished by the end of the war, there could still be difficulties for those who had taken that stand. Muriel McMillan believed that many COs 'made considerable sacrifices. I know of a number who lost their jobs, some who had families and lost their jobs; there was also of course the uncertainty of what would happen to them when the war ended, how they would be regarded, whether they would be able to get jobs again. In some cases, I am sure it changed their lives completely.'

Mervyn Taggert in an interview with the Imperial War Museum said that it was hard to find work after the war: 'Quite rightly, jobs went to the ex-servicemen … it was more difficult for people who had been COs … At the start of the war I lost my job because of it and after the war it was difficult because naturally the servicemen got the jobs and the training grants.' Denis Hayes too, who had spent the war years working with the CBCO also felt that 'People found doors were closed to them that had previously been open. No explanation was given but they knew what it was … I was pretty popular when I was a youngster and I found it quite a serious problem to find that there was always a black mark against me.'

Eric Farley too encountered some difficulties after the war. According to his daughter, Susannah: 'Later on in life, he applied to become a prison visitor and there was still prejudice against people who had been COs during the war. I suppose that would have been in the '60s. He was just excluded because he'd been a CO and of course he'd been in prison.' Denis Allen, who had served time in Feltham, Wandsworth Prison and Wormwood Scrubs, had a similar experience. He applied for a job in the prison service, which he did not get even though Fenner Brockway wrote on his behalf, and he was similarly turned down when he applied for a job in an approved school.

Back to work

To his amazement, Edward Blishen, who by the time the war ended was working on the land with German prisoners of war, was offered a permanent job with the War Agricultural Committee. He refused: 'I felt very dizzy indeed. For the first time for nearly six years I was being actually solicited, sought after, offered a choice … But any sense I might have had of the luxury of it foundered in my sense of its grotesqueness.' Instead, he applied for, and was offered, a teaching job with a school in Hampstead. He published his first book in 1955 and eventually gave up teaching to become a full-time writer and broadcaster.

Given their principles, it is not surprising that many COs went into socially useful work after the war. Kathleen Wigham, who had gone to prison for her beliefs, became a home tutor for children with learning and other difficulties. She died in September 2010 and according to Quaker testimony given when she died, it was work that she loved. She also helped to develop the signing system known as Makaton, which is used extensively with children and adults with special needs. Brian Phillips, having spent the war years working on the land, went into teaching. After the war Joan Pasco worked at the War Resisters' International (WRI) headquarters in Enfield, helping them in their work to unite war resisters worldwide. Subsequently she worked with the Shop Workers' Union. Ifanwy Williams continued in social work and was still closely involved with the Fellowship of Reconciliation (FoR) in 2010, when I was fortunate enough to meet her.

Stella St John was still working with the FoR when war in Europe ended and was attending an FoR conference in Wales on VE Day. There were no celebrations: 'well, you were absolutely delighted of course but … there was so much trouble still around I don't think you felt like celebrating so much with refugees and all of starving Europe.' Following the end of the war, she continued full-time with her work at the Hungerford Club.

Eric Farley who, to quote his daughter, was 'a man of many parts', did a number of different things after the war. Having been in prison, at Holton-cum-Beckering and the Mellanby scabies project during the war, when it ended he returned to his pre-war local government job in Battersea even though he had been dismissed in 1940. In his mid-fifties he retrained as a teacher at Sydney Webb College, and then, after retirement, went to the Shakespeare Institution at Stratford on Avon, where he did an MA in Shakespearean studies. Clearly literature, which had helped him get through his time in the guardroom and in Lewes Prison, was an abiding love.

Fred Vahey, who was also an artist, and his wife Zoe, who also painted but became engrossed in archaeology and the Celts, continued working their smallholding, 'Innisfree', in Pett, Sussex until their deaths, aiming as much as possible for a non-exploitative self-sufficiency. They consistently welcomed peace groups, making their land available to among others the Woodcraft Folk, who camped there regularly.

Doubts and pressures

To have taken a stand as a conscientious objector during the Second World War was an enormous step, and one that ran absolutely contrary to what the vast majority of people were doing both on the home front and in the forces abroad. Refusing to fight while bombs were falling on London, Liverpool, Coventry and other cities was not an easy decision, nor was living with the knowledge of what was happening in Nazi Germany.

Not everyone who registered as a conscientious objector during the Second World War maintained the same stand through to the end. Some changed their minds for personal or social reasons, feeling that it was no longer appropriate to be a conscientious objector when the world was at war. Francis Cammaerts was one who did so, even though in his book *A Pacifist at War*, he maintains that fundamentally he remained a pacifist. Others included the sculptor and painter Sven Berlin, who was later part of the St Ives group of artists. He registered as a conscientious objector and worked in the garden of a big house outside St Ives, owned by the art critic Adrian Stokes. He changed his mind; according to his obituary in the *Independent* (17 December 1999) this was because he saw some distressing naval bombing in the Channel, and joined the army, taking part in the D-Day landing. The experience led to a nervous breakdown. By contrast, two other artists from the St Ives group, Bryan Wynter and Patrick Heron, who also registered as COs, stuck to their stand. Both Wynter and Heron were directed to land work. In Heron's case, three years' heavy agricultural work intensified the asthma that he had had since childhood but he had refused to declare for exemption.

Another who had a change of mind and heart was Clifford Simmons. His father had fought in the First World and was killed at Passchendaele in 1917, when Clifford was only three years old. His mother died not long after. These events, combined with his political and Christian beliefs, led him to become active in the inter-war peace movement. When war arrived he registered as a conscientious objector and was initially directed into a non-combatant unit. Clifford did not accept this, not being prepared to 'release another to apply the force which I myself would not sanction' but on appeal was given unconditional exemption. He worked with civil defence during the London Blitz, feeling that he was making some contribution to 'mitigating the effects of war'. After a while, being aware of what was happening to Jews in Germany and those who were opposing Hitler, Clifford felt he could no longer 'stand aside from the struggle which was engulfing my contemporaries'. In May 1942 he joined the Royal Armoured Corps and in June 1944 took part in the Normandy landings.

Those who abandoned their stand as conscientious objectors were in a minority and there were also a few who, having enlisted in the armed forces, subsequently switched to becoming conscientious objectors. However, most of those who made the decision to conscientiously object to taking up arms or contributing to the military machine stuck by their decision, no matter how difficult it was at times. Some had no shadow of doubt about the decision they had made. Fred Vahey never doubted his decision, even when his elder brother died in an Italian prisoner of war camp – perhaps for him it just emphasised the futility of war. His wife Zoe though did question her absolute pacifism after the war, when she heard of the concentration camps and according to her daughter Lorna wondered whether, if she had known, she would have maintained her absolutism.

Kenneth Wray, who was also an absolutist and equally horrified by the slaughter of Jews, felt that war itself had caused their deaths. A profound believer in the power of non-violence, he had read the writings of Bart de Ligt, a Dutchman and proponent of non-violence, who had supported conscientious objectors during the First World War, and thought: 'He said, " … You can defeat your enemy by non-violence." He put it out in absolute detail exactly what everyone should do … Jews would not have been killed had it not been for the war. It was the war which allowed Hitler to shoot or gas all those Jews. He couldn't have done it in a peaceful world, but because of war he could just exterminate them.'

Reading through personal accounts and listening to interviews, there is no doubt that with Britain and her allies at war with Nazism, and with the mobilisation of the entire British population for total war, there were moments when some conscientious objectors felt guilty about their stand. Feeling isolated and separated from peers and the general community did not help. In Tony Parker's experience: 'I think you did feel very alone, or at least I did. Most conchies did because it was never a clear-cut issue; all the time one was saying "Am I doing right or am I doing wrong?" "Ought I to rethink this?" Especially if you had a friend who was killed or injured. That was the time you felt really rather bad about it, guilty about it … One would meet people who'd say, "We've just won the battle of something or other," you felt separate from that I think.'

Sydney Carter also felt ambivalent. In a piece that he wrote about his experience as a conscientious objector, he describes a particular day when 'my mind went one way, shouting all the intellectual arguments for pacifism, my heart (or something) spun off in the opposite direction. Which one was I? The division was unbearable … For about a day I wandered, one half of me already in the recruiting office. Right or wrong, I was part of the society that fed and clothed me … Like the prodigal, I wanted to come home again, submit and be received into the big, warm bosom of Society.' Serving with the Friends Ambulance Unit (FAU) helped to resolve his ambivalence and he maintained his conscientious stand throughout the war. He was not the only one to feel this internal split; many COs felt like outsiders, which to a great extent they were. It is little wonder that COs with the Pacifist Service Units identified with the socially disadvantaged that they were working with.

It is probably true to say, as one CO has, that the Second World War was not an easy war to oppose. By definition, conscientious objectors were in the main thoughtful people with social consciences: refusing to be conscripted to fight Fascism and Nazism was a dilemma. Edward Blishen in his book *Cack-handed War* mentions 'the awful guilt of standing aside'. Others too were very aware of how much easier it was for them to take their stand in a democratic society while citizenship, freedom of expression and individualism were being ruthlessly repressed in Nazi Germany.

When Eric Farley returned to his office after his appeal tribunal there was some 'discussion at work among those responsible for the payment of salaries about whether I should be docked for being absent to attend an appellate tribunal, which I only had the right and not the necessity to appear before. This debate was inbred with trace elements of resentment and animosity, which was almost entirely confined to the older men whose own war, in which some had suffered greatly, was only 20 years before. One was also made aware … of the privilege of dissent accorded by a democracy but certainly not by Nazi Germany where the unimaginable rigours of the concentration camps were the least a pacifist might be subject to. It was uncomfortable knowledge to live with.'

Then and even now, the argument was put forward that, given the awfulness of the Nazi regime, the Second World War could have been regarded as a 'just' war but despite any doubts they may have had, conscientious objectors could not accept this. To fight and kill was unacceptable; for them there had to be another way. As Tony Parker said: 'I could never distinguish between a just and unjust killing – it's not just to kill anyone at any time whatsoever.'

Never wavered

Despite times of self-doubt, conscientious objectors believed profoundly that it was wrong to take up arms and engage in killing, and most never wavered. In his interview with the Imperial War Museum, Kenneth Wray said, 'It was difficult, the sense of isolation, [being] completely alone [but] … as far as I was concerned, I was going to stand absolutely solid and nothing would shake me.' Muriel McMillan felt the same and believed that she and her husband Arthur helped each other through: 'I was helped by Arthur's own strength and convictions. I think we helped each other. I didn't waver; whether I would have done so if I had had to undergo what Arthur went through I don't know, but I was never put to the test. Many times in his letters, Arthur refers to the strength of fellowship, the fact that he is being given the grace to maintain his witness and he is greatly helped too by a letter he had from a conscientious objector in the First World War in which he says: "Always remember that Man can do nothing to you unless it is allowed by God" and that I'm sure helped him on many occasions.'

Support from other COs was invaluable; Edward Blishen thought that 'inevitably, conchies developed a very great sense of loyalty to the unpopular group they formed. In the first great war, they had been martyrised: in this one they were put into positions of obscure discomfort. Both kinds of fate held the dissidents together, powerfully.' Clearly, not all conscientious objectors, being as highly individual as they were, and often having very different political, social and religious reasons for their stand, did not always get on harmoniously any more than any other disparate group of people. Nevertheless they helped each whenever they could, not least through journals, meetings, work placements and via organisations such as the PPU and the CBCO.

Like many COs Tony Parker sometimes felt that people misunderstood his pacifism: 'I always thought I was very patriotic. I remember at the time of Dunkirk or the Battle of Britain, some man who came into the shop … he was a clergyman … around Manchester there is some very beautiful scenery and … he asked me to go walking with him, which I did. We stood and looked at the countryside and then he suddenly turned to me and he said: "Don't you think this is worth defending?" And this is a common mistake I think people make with pacifists; they think that pacifists don't believe in defending things, it's really a matter of method, it's not a matter of you don't resist, it's a matter of a different way of resisting ... and I said to him, "Yes, I do feel this is worth defending but I certainly do not agree that killing people or attacking people is the right way to defend it".'

Achievements

The number of conscientious objectors during the Second World War was far greater than 20 years previously although compared with the numbers who enlisted in the armed forces it was small: 66,000 or so compared with around eight million but despite their small numbers they had a considerable impact. The First World War conscientious objectors had blazed a path for their predecessors, gaining them some sort of acceptance, however grudging and reluctant it was. Second World War COs did not therefore have to fight for the right to exist. Instead they made a different contribution – they showed that it was possible for individuals to stand up against state control and to challenge the prevailing militarism. They set an impressive example.

In his book *Challenge of Conscience* Denis Hayes makes some very interesting observations. He says, as do many others, that COs of the Second World War had a much easier time than their predecessors. They did suffer: 'Many lost their jobs; some went to prison for their beliefs. Others were victimised by society in a subtle way ... But ... the burden was comparatively light.'

Victimisation, although it existed, was less than it had been and options for non-militaristic service to the community were far greater, which in some ways reduced the threat that the objectors' stand might otherwise have presented. There was a gap between COs and the wider society but in Hayes's opinion, the 'superb confidence of the earlier generation with its crusading vigour had given way to an altogether quieter and less evangelical type'. Those who had faced up to the harsh realities of Nazism knew that their stand would not solve the problems of the war so they had to work in other ways. The COs' struggle shifted 'from opposing conscription to maintaining the right to individual objection ... ' and, in Denis Hayes's opinion they 'brought a quiet but unmistakable moral leadership in moves that may virtually affect the future of society'.

The pioneering social work of the Pacifist Service Units, the service of the Friends Ambulance Unit and a host of other humanitarian contributions on the home front or abroad, helping in the Blitz, fighting fires, driving ambulances, involvement in bomb disposal were, by the end of the war certainly acknowledged, so on a practical level, their non-violent contribution to relieving the suffering of war was widely recognised. Many also went on to work with refugees and the displaced of the post-war world. COs won respect for their humanitarian work. But most significant was the stand they took. At a time when the world was at war, more than 60,000 individuals refused to fight because their consciences would not allow them to do so. They proved it was possible to stand up against state control, providing a moral and prinicipled example and highlighting the need to find alternatives to war, not an easy stand at the time. The effects of their actions continued well after the war ended and still find expression in the peace movement to this day.

Fenner Brockway once said that 'The conscientious objector has no right to reject war in the present unless he spends his life in helping to make a future without war' and most COs did not stop their work for peace once war was over. The horror of atomic warfare and the threat of nuclear destruction took many of them into the Campaign for Nuclear Disarmament (CND) and other anti-war organisations, and although a nuclear war would, by definition, not involve war on the ground in the same way as the previous world wars, they nevertheless continued putting whatever effort they could into trying to create a world free of war. On an individual level too, former COs speak at public meetings, write books or articles and do what they can to encourage others to reject militarism and war. They no longer need to challenge conscription but the need for them to promote their beliefs has not gone away.

On an international level, the determination of conscientious objectors has had an impact, influencing American draft dodgers during the Vietnam War and highlighting the situation of Israeli refuseniks currently serving prison sentences for refusing to be conscripted. More recently the case of the anti-Afghan War soldier Joe Glenton, who was imprisoned in 2010 for refusing to fight, received considerable press coverage. Britain has not re-introduced conscription since 1960 and other countries have slowly followed suit, particularly in Europe. In 1987 the United Nations Commission on Human Rights recognised 'the right of everyone to have conscientious objection to military service as a legitimate exercise of the right of freedom, thought, and religion'. In 2001 the Council of Europe Parliamentary

Assembly recommended that the right of conscientious objection be incorporated into the European Convention on Human Rights. Five member states— Albania, Armenia, Azerbaijan, Macedonia and Turkey – do not recognise the rights of conscientious objectors, but conscription has been abolished in Belgium, Holland, Luxembourg and Spain and is being phased out in France and Italy.

The tradition of conscientious objection against militarism finds expression in other areas as well. In 2005 a group of 'conscientious objectors' campaigned to prevent the government from using taxes to fund the Iraq War; they lost their fight but individuals held back a percentage of their tax as a conscientious objection to allowing their money to be used for war. Others refuse to take jobs linked to the military, and particularly involvement in weapons research and development. The CBCO continued its work well after the Second World War, supporting conscientious objectors to National Service who refused to fight in Korea and Suez until its role was effectively taken over by the Peace Pledge Union. The PPU to this day still works for peace and to highlight the situation of unwilling combatants and continuing conflicts worldwide. The Fellowship of Reconciliation, War Resisters' International, Women's International League of Peace and Freedom to say nothing of smaller organisations also continue to this day.

Pride

On a personal level, individual conscientious objectors have made a very positive impact. Fred Vahey's daughter, Lorna, acknowledges a deep debt to her father and has been active in the peace movement for most of her adult life. She and I have marched and demonstrated against a series of wars, from Vietnam through to Iraq, and together cut wire at Greenham Common, losing a very expensive pair of wire cutters in the process.

Asked about the impact of her father's stand, she says: 'I think there was pride … it was always hammered into us, well not hammered but he talked about it such a lot that there was never any idea that you could possibly think another way. I think most things you just sort of grow to imbibe, they are the norm. Painting pictures was the norm; not doing as you were told was the norm, being a conscientious objector was the norm, so you grow up thinking this is the way you behave.' Lorna has no doubt that her father's stand and her parents' actions helped to shape her anti-war views: 'I didn't ever have to think about it. They had to think about it, reason about where they were going to stand. I just didn't have to, it was so obvious.' An artist, she continues to contribute to the anti-war movement with beautifully designed banners and artworks

Susannah Farley Green too, whom I first met when she was an activist with the Robertsbridge Peace Council, remembers the impact her father's stand had on her: 'I remember the weirdest thing was when I was about nine, I was walking around on Remembrance Day and the guns went off on Wimbledon Common and these two old ladies who were walking down the street, stopped, hung their heads and stood there and I carried on going. I didn't do anything at all. They came up to me and said how badly behaved I was. And I said: "Why, what have I done wrong?" They told me and I went back home and Dad said, "Well, that's the difference." ... Many years later we used to go on demonstrations and sit in Grosvenor Square ... as a family, it was brilliant.' Although today Susannah does not accept her father's attitude to Remembrance Day, believing that it is important to remember the dead of both world wars, she remains powerfully anti-war and has a considerable pride in both her father and uncle: 'It's the pride in them ... It's a bit like having someone who was highly decorated.'

When asked if they would take the same stand again, most conscientious objectors say they would, with perhaps a few changes. Mervyn Taggert would have certainly have registered as a conscientious objector but in retrospect felt he had been wrong to stick to an absolutist position during the war: 'On balance I think I took the wrong attitude, that I would have nothing to do with the war effort. I remember a woman doctor saying, "Why don't you go into the hospital service during the war?" I didn't because it seemed to be in support of the war effort ... With the wisdom of hindsight, I can see that this was wrong ... The idea of saving life is right in itself and an overriding consideration. I think many pacifists went too far in this uncooperative attitude'.

Tony Parker went on to be a writer and playwright. He wrote a programme about conscientious objectors, during the course of which he interviewed a number of COs: 'I think the thing that struck me most was ... what a lot of bloody awkward sods they all were, they were all just as obdurate as I am. One of the questions I asked them was, "If it could occur again, would you do exactly the same thing?" and they all said "Yes". When I asked them, "Is there anything you would do differently, they all gave exactly the same answer I would have given … they all came out with exactly what my answer would have been 40 years later … If anyone had asked me the question, I would have said: "Yes, if it would reoccur and looking back on it, I wouldn't have gone to a tribunal. I wouldn't have said I'm going to explain to you why I'm a pacifist and why I'm a conscientious objector. I would have said: "I'm a conscientious objector, I'm not going to take part in this way, you must do whatever you feel is necessary and I'm not even going to explain it to you." And they all said exactly the same.'

Bibliography and References

Barker, Rachel, *Conscience, Government and War: Conscientious Objection in Great Britain 1939–45*, (Routledge & Kegan Paul, 1982).

Blishen, Edward, *A Cack-handed War*, (Thames & Hudson, 1972).

Braithwaite, Constance, *Conscientious Objection to Compulsions Under the Law*, (William Sessions Ltd, 1995).

Brock, Peter ed., *'These Strange Criminals': An Anthology of Prison Memoirs by Conscientious Objectors from the Great War to the Cold War*, (University of Toronto Press, 2004).

Brock, Peter and Socknat, Thomas Paul, *Challenge to Mars: Essays on Pacifism from 1918 to 1945*, (University of Toronto Press, 1999).

Brock, Peter and Young, Nigel, *Pacifism in the Twentieth Century*, (University of Toronto Press Inc, 1999).

Ceadel, Martin, *Pacifism in Britain 1914–1945: The Defining of a Faith*, (Clarendon Press, 1980).

Davies, A Tegla, *Friends Ambulance Unit: The Story of the F.A.U. in the Second World War 1939–1946*, (George Allen and Unwin Ltd, 1947).

Elster, Ellen and Serensen, Majken Jul, *Women Conscientious Objectors: An Anthology*, (War Resisters' International, 2010).

Farley, Eric, *A Partial View: 31.12.1940 -5.1941*, (unpublished memoir, 1983).

Fussell, Paul, *The Great War and Modern Memory*, (Oxford University Press, 1975).

Gaffin, Jean & Thomas, David, *Caring & Sharing: The Centenary History of the Co-operative Women's Guild*, (Co-operative Union Ltd, 1983).

Goodall, Felicity, *A Question of Conscience: Conscientious Objection in the two World Wars*, (Sutton Publishing, 1997).

Hardinge Pritchard, C, *In My Grave I am Not*, (New Millennium, 1998).

Hayes, Denis, *Challenge of Conscience: The Story of the Conscientious Objectors of 1939–1949*, (Allen and Unwin, 1949).

Hayes, Denis, *Conscription Conflict*, (Sheppard Press, 1949).

Hetherington, William, *Swimming Against the Tide: the Peace Pledge Union story 1934–2009*, (Peace Pledge Union, 2009).

Huxley, Aldous, *Ends and Means: An Enquiry into the Nature of Ideals and into the Methods Employed for their Realization*, (Chatto & Windus, 1937).

Mellanby, Kenneth, *Human Guinea Pigs*, (Merlin Press, 1973).

Morrison, Sybil, *I Renounce War: The Story of the Peace Pledge Union*, (Sheppard Press, 1962).

Sheppard, H.R.L., *We Say "No": The Plain Man's Guide to Pacifism*, (John Murray, 1935).

Simmons, Clifford, *The Objectors: The personal story of five conscientious objectors*, (Times Press, 1965).

Smith, Lyn, *Voices Against War: A Century of Protest*, (Mainstream Publishing Co, 2009).

Voices: References

Imperial War Museum (IWM) Sound Archives:

Extracts taken from the following IWM sound archives, which are housed in the Imperial War Museum. The name of the person quoted is followed by the IWM catalogue number and date of interview (in brackets).

Allen, Denis: 11522 (1990)
Beavor, Douglas: 4788 (1980)
Bing, Harold: 358 (1974)
Bottini, Reginald: 4660 (1980)
Bramwell, James: 9542 (1986)
Brockway, Fenner: 476 (1974)
Eddington, Paul: 9328 (1986)
Elliot, William: 7108 (1983)
Gibson, Tony: 12267 (1991)
Goldring, Ernest: 4658 (1980)
Hardie, Leslie: 12179 (1991)
Hayes, Denis: 4828 (1981)
Hayley, Tom: 10143 (1988)
Mallone, Ronald: 4581 (1980)
McMillan, Arthur: *see* McMillian, Muriel
McMillan, Muriel 'Babs': 4829 (1981)
Newcombe, Vic: 9400 (1986)
Nicholls, Doris: 4634 (1980)
Parker, Tony: 9233 (1986)
Pasco, Joan: 4507 (1979)
Petts, John: 9732 (1987)
Sharp, Peter: 30340 (2008)

Soper, Donald: 12790 (1992)
St John, Stella: 4997 (1971)
Swann, Donald: 9133 (1985)
Taggart, Mervyn: 4657 (1980)
Wigham, Kathleen: 4761 (1980)
Wray, Kenneth: 4696 (1980)

Interviews
Brian Phillips
Ifanway Williams
Susannah Farley Green: memories of her father Eric Farley
Lorna Vahey : memories of her father Fred Vahey
Jane Foot & Gwylim Newnham: memories of their father Jack Newnham

Imperial War Museum: Documents
Bunnewell, L.F. IWM 10829 P355
Hope-Gill, C.W. IWM 80/7/1
Huzzard, Ron IWM 4702
Iveson, Stan IWM Cat 80/7/1
Morel, F. IWM 4699 80/7/1
Porcas, RJ. IWM 10/2/1
St John, Stella IWM 83/7/1

BBC *The People's War*
Martin Davies
Ronald Smith
Bragg, Billy, *The Conchies of Holton-cum-Beckering*, (BBC Radio 4, 27 May 2009).

Journals And Newspapers
Hastings and St Leonards Observer
The *Independent*
The *Guardian*
Peace News, with thanks to the Peace Pledge Union for permission to quote.
The Times
The Tribunal (journal of the Fellowship of Conscientious Objectors)
CBCO *Bulletin*

Pamphlets

Abundance of Creation, Michael Tippet, *Peace News*, 1944 (second edition 1975, Housmans).

Peace Service Handbook, (Peace Pledge Union, 1939).

The C.O. and the Tribunal, (Joint Advisory Bureau, undated / c.1939).

The London Tribunal questions the C.O., (London Friends' Local Conscription Committee, 1939).

Archive Material

Mass Observation, *Conscientious Objection and Pacifism 1939–44*

Peace Pledge Union: with many thanks for permission to quote from *Challenge of Conscience* by Denis Hayes, and from the PPU website.

The Imperial War Museum: Sound Archives and Document Section

Hansard

Websites

BBC WW2 People's War: conscientious objectors
www.bbc.co.uk/history/ww2peopleswar/categories/c1173

Peace Pledge Union (PPU): CO Project
www.coproject.org.uk

Women's Peace Pilgrimage 1926: news clip
www.britishpathe.com/record.php?id=25379

Index